THE
FLOWER GARDEN

SUMMER FLOWERS FROM SEED

THE
FLOWER GARDEN

SUMMER FLOWERS FROM SEED

ALAN TOOGOOD

CRESCENT BOOKS
NEW YORK

Executive Managers	Kelly Flynn
	Susan Egerton-Jones
Art Editor	Sue Hall
Production	Peter Phillips

1987 Edition published by Crescent Books,
distributed by Crown Publishers, Inc.

Created in association with Unwins (Seeds) Ltd
Edited and designed by the Artists House
Division of Mitchell Beazley International Ltd
Artists House
14–15 Manette Street
London W1V 5LB

An Artists House Book
© Mitchell Beazley Publishers 1987

ISBN 0-517-62187-8

Typeset by Hourds Typographica, Stafford.
Reproduction by La Cromolito s.n.c., Milan.
Printed in Spain by Printer Industria Grafica SA, Barcelona.
D.L.B. 811-1987

h g f e d c b a

Contents

*I*ntroduction

There is no faster way of providing masses of colour in a garden than raising hardy annuals, half-hardy annuals and hardy biennials from seed. These are the plants which form the basis of this book.

All are short-term plants – that is, they are discarded when their display is over. Most are grown for colourful flowers although some are noted for spectacular foliage. Leaf colour and interest should not be ignored in planting schemes for it makes a marvellous contrast for blooms.

As most plants in these three groups are easily raised from seed they have special appeal to newcomers to gardening while many advanced gardeners grow a good range of them as a matter of course.

Annuals complete their life cycle within one growing season. They grow from seed, produce their blooms, set a crop of seeds and then they die. All of this takes place well within one year. Some annuals live for only a few months, others for many months and generally we use those annuals with the longest life cycles for our garden displays.

Hardy annuals (HA) are able to survive frosts and cold weather to a greater or lesser extent according to species and the part of the world from which they originate. These are sown out of doors direct in their flowering positions between early and late spring. The hardiest of the hardy annuals can also be sown in the autumn. They overwinter as small plants and flower earlier the following year, than if they were sown in the spring. The majority of hardy annuals bloom in the summer.

Half-hardy annuals (HHA) are frost sensitive and will be damaged or killed if subjected to frosts. In climates with cold winters (and hence frosts) half-hardy annuals are raised in a frost-free environment in winter or spring (according to species) and are planted out in their flowering positions when all danger of frost is over. They flower throughout summer and into autumn but the display will be stopped by the first frosts of autumn.

Among the half-hardy annuals included here are some plants which are, correctly, perennials (plants which live for a number of years). However, they are more successfully grown when treated as half-hardy annuals anywhere which is not sub-tropical.

Half-hardy annuals are popularly called summer bedding plants. This is due to the fact that they are 'bedded out' (planted) for summer display.

Biennials take two growing seasons to complete their life cycle. In year one they are sown, usually in spring or early summer, and they grow for the rest of that year, overwintering outdoors. In year two they flower, in spring or summer according to species; then they set a crop of seeds and die. The hardy biennials (HB), the ones we are dealing with here, generally survive cold winters without protection, although some, like wallflowers, will not come through really severe winter weather without protection and cannot be overwintered outdoors in many parts of the USA. A few hardy perennials and also included under this heading because they are treated as biennials by gardeners. In theory these are capable of living for a number of years although they would quickly decline in vigour if kept.

Some of the spring-flowering biennials are popularly called spring bedding plants.

Why we grow these plants

Colour is the most important characteristic of the annuals and biennials so if you want masses of colour in your garden they should top the list of desirable plants. They are mass planted to provide really bold splashes of colour – to create great impact. These plants cannot be used sparingly – we want plenty of them, but this need not be expensive if you raise your own from seed.

Nowadays, it is, of course, possible to buy a wide variety of ready-to-plant half-hardy annuals and hardy biennials at garden centres and nurseries. They come in boxes or trays and sometimes in pots, ready for planting out. Spring sees the garden centres well-stocked with summer bedding plants while autumn is the time to buy plants for spring bedding.

Seeds are cheap, comparatively and packets of seeds of many of the plants described and illustrated in this book will be found in garden centres and shops in the winter and spring. The more unusual species and varieties will have to be bought mail-order from seedsmen, who produce colourful and informative annual catalogues. Once you get on to the mailing lists of seedsmen and place an order you will automatically receive their catalogues each year – generally they are mailed in the autumn.

Some plants are easier to raise than others. Sowing hardy annuals and biennials direct in the open ground is straightforward enough and reommended for complete beginners. Raising plants from seeds in a greenhouse calls for a little more skill but most gardeners find they can quickly master it.

Annuals and biennials have many uses in the garden. Hardy annuals can be grown in their own special border; they can be used to fill gaps in mixed borders containing shrubs and hardy perennials; while small varieties can be used to provide colour on rock gardens and in paving.

Half-hardy annuals are normally used for more formal summer bedding displays, for example around the house, patio or terrace; they can be used to fill containers – urns, tubs, window boxes and hanging baskets – with summer colour; and they can also be used to fill spaces in mixed borders.

Some of the hardy biennials are used for formal spring bedding displays; others look at home in a cottage-garden border, perhaps alongside some hardy annuals; while some can be used to fill gaps in mixed borders. Spring bedding plants are also excellent for ornamental containers.

Some of the larger more dramatic plants can be used as focal points or accent plants to create different profiles and to lead the eye to some particular part. Good use, too, can be made of climbing plants clothing walls and fences, and there are several climbing hardy annuals to choose from.

Some of the plants selected here are excellent for cut flowers. A few could be grown specially for cutting in a spare part of the garden.

Site Planning

Suitable Sites

The majority of plants here should be sown or planted in full sun or in positions which are in shade for only a small part of the day. There are some annuals and biennials which will also grow well in partial shade. Nevertheless, even these do enjoy some sunshine. Dappled shade as created by trees is an example of partial shade. Another example is a bed or border which receives sun for only about half the day.

If the full sun-loving plants are grown in shady spots they will become straggly and produce few if any flowers.

Most plants prefer a sheltered position, free from cold drying winds. Cold winter winds can cause a lot of damage to young plants by ''scorching'' their foliage, high winds in summer, often coupled with rain, can flatten tall thin-stemmed plants such as many of the hardy annuals. Bear in mind that less staking or supporting is necessary in a wind-sheltered garden.

Shelter can be provided by hedges and shrubs, and larger gardens can be protected by tall windbreaks of deciduous or evergreen trees or conifers. Temporary wind protection can also be used until permanent plantings become established. Windbreak netting supported on a system of wooden posts and horizontal wires can be every effective.

The Principles of Using Colour

The main reason for growing annuals and biennials is to provide masses of colour. Indeed one could say that this book is basically about creating colour with plants. But some thought has to be given to the use of colour just as it is when decorating one's rooms. Some people have a natural flare for this, being able to combine colours to great effect; others are not so blessed. But there is no need for them to despair, because happily in nature few colours clash or look absolutely awful together, so the risk of making serious mistakes is minimal.

Hopefully, though, I can tell you enough about using colour to enable you to get down to planning some delightful colour schemes for your beds and borders.

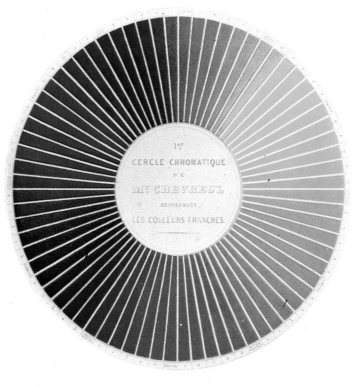

The Colour Wheel

The colour wheel will help you to combine colours effectively and can be used as a guide when planning your planting schemes. It comprises the three primary colours – red, blue and yellow. Between these are the intermediate colours which are obtained by mixing the primary colours. You could put this to the practical test by 'playing around' with a box of artist's watercolour paints.

On the colour wheel all complementary colours (those which combine well) face one another. To quote a few examples, red complements green, blue complements orange, yellow complements violet, and so on with the intermediate colours.

The paler shades of all these colours (including pastel colours) are obtained by mixing white with them (again experiment with your box of paints). For instance, pink is obtained by mixing white with red. Darker shades of the primary and intermediate colours are obtained by mixing black with them.

Harmony

Going a step further we should aim for colours which
harmonize and/or contrast when planning planting
schemes.

Subtle and 'restful' effects are achieved by combining
harmonizing colours. But what are these?

They are the closest colours on the colour wheel – the
closer the colours the better they harmonize. Thus we could
combine the blue flowers of anchusas and lobelias with the
blue-violets of heliotropes and pansies and the violet of
Verbena venosa; or red-violet petunias with red *Salvia spendens*
and orange-red amaranthus.

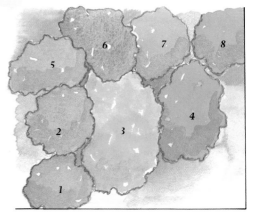

HARMONY

1 *Pansies*
2 *Lobelia erinus*
3 *Heliotrope*
4 *Petunia 'Plum Picotee'*
5 *Verbena venosa*
6 *Anchusa capensis*
7 *Salvia splendens*
8 *Amaranthus tricolor*

Contrast

Contrasting colours create more dramatic effects and are used if you want your beds and borders to have real impact. Looking at the colour wheel, examples of contrasting colours are blue and orange, which could be obtained by mixing blue nigella and convolvulus with orange calendulas or marigolds; yellow and violet (try yellow antirrhinums and African marigolds with violet heliotrope); and orange-yellow and blue-violet (try wallflowers and pansies in these colours).

Beware of overdoing planting schemes with contrasting colours – too many beds and borders planned in this way could result in a very unrestful garden.

CONTRAST

1 *Convolvulous tricolor*
2 *Calendula officinalis*
3 *Nigella damascena*
4 *Wallflowers*
5 *Pansies*
6 *Antirrhinums*
7 *Heliotrope*
8 *African Marigold*

Using Colour Effectively

Each colour is capable of creating a 'mood' or atmosphere in a garden. Let's take a look at each colour and assess the effect it creates.

Green This is an important colour – indeed the basic colour of most gardens, provided by a permanent 'framework' of shrubs, trees, hedges and lawns. This green framework makes an excellent background and foil for brighter colours. You may think that a lot of green gives a dull effect but this is not so, for there are many 'greens': light, medium and dark; blue-greens; grey-greens; bronze-greens; silver-greens; and yellow-greens.

Green creates a cool restful atmosphere which is what most people desire in a garden. There are green-flowered annuals which could be used to further create this effect. Green-flowered plants are also useful for separating strong colours such as reds and scarlets.

White, silver and grey These create a cool atmosphere, and there are quite a few plants with white flowers and several with silver or grey foliage; all are extremely useful and should be used freely. Mix these plants with strong, dark or heavy colours to prevent a sombre or too powerful effect; use them also to lighten dark areas. They can be used with any other colour without fear of clashing and are especially useful for keeping apart strong colours.

Yellow This is a cheerful colour, bringing 'sunshine' to the garden. Dramatic contrasts can be created by combining with bright yellow such colours as violet, blue or purple; red or orange is often combined with yellow to create tremendous impact. Pale shades of yellow look lovely with strong purples, blues and violets.

Yellow really shows up in a garden and can be seen from a considerable distance; it is also very conspicuous at dusk.

Orange This is one of the colours that creates a 'warm' atmosphere in a garden, as do the yellows and reds. Indeed orange is a mixture of the two.

You can create a dramatic contrast by combining orange with blue. It can also be used with reds and yellows to create a really powerful effect. Like yellow, orange can be seen from a great distance.

Red This is a hot colour, useful for creating 'warmth' in a cool climate – particularly on dull summer days. Green complements red, which comes in several shades such as scarlet, orange and crimson (on the blue side). If you intend using a lot of red flowers provide a foil of green, white, silver or grey blooms and/or foliage. A large area of red without this relief can be overpowering. Try not to scatter red around the garden too much but keep it in one or two places. This ensures a more restful garden – you don't really want to 'see red' wherever you look.

Pink There are many shades of pink, on the blue side of red and on the orange side. It is an easy colour to use and very restful in the paler shades. It gives a warmish feeling to a planting scheme. Pale pinks look lovely with blues and yellow in pastel shades. Pinks of all shades combine beautifully with white, grey and silver. Use the shades of pink with blue in them with blue flowers, and the pinks with orange in them with orange or yellow flowers.

Purple and violet These are 'heavy' colours and if used on too large a scale can create a sombre effect. They come between red and blue on the colour wheel and can be used with both of them. Pale versions are mauve and lilac.

Purples and violets combine well with yellows and oranges, too. Some lovely effects can be created by combining whites and pale yellows with purple and violet flowers. Use white or pale yellow to separate these two deep colours from other strong colours if required.

Blue A lovely colour for a warm or hot climate, blue creates a cool atmosphere. Nevertheless it is also used a lot in cooler climates. For a dramatic contrast combine blue with orange. To liven up groups of blue flowers combine with them plants with yellow or white blooms. The blues blend well with purples and violets, but you should avoid overdoing it because it can create a sombre effect. A stimulating effect, bordering on a clashing combination, is blue and red. This is all too often overdone in summer bedding schemes; using red salvias or geraniums with blue lobelia looks quite good, but *not* everywhere!

Perspective

You can use colours to create illusions in the garden: for example, to make a border look longer or shorter. Pale colours create a sense of distance because they cannot be seen too clearly. Strong bright colours have the opposite effect because they are seen clearly and appear to be closer to you.

To make a border appear longer than it really is use pale colours at the far end such as the whites, silvers, greys and pastel shades of blues, mauves and yellows. At the near end of the border use the strongest colours: purples, reds, scarlet, oranges, crimson and dark blues. A border can be made to look shorter by reversing the colours.

Beds planted with very pale flowers at the far end of a garden will create the illusion of distance. Pale specimen plants used as focal points will do the same – a good plant for this purpose is the Scotch thistle or *Onopordum*.

Restricted Use of Colours

Although they run in and out of fashion, borders consisting of plants in shades of one colour, or perhaps two colours, can be effective. You may not want to devote an entire large border to this so try it out in part of a border, or devote a small bed to a single-colour scheme.

RED BORDER

1 *Ricinus communis 'Gibsonii'*
2 *Coix lacryma-jobi*
3 *Dahlias*
4 *Canna*
5 *Nicotiana 'Domino Scarlet'*
6 *Linum grandiflorum*
7 *Briza maxima*
8 *Kochia scoparia trichophila*

Red border A lovely, warm scheme can be created with red, but don't make too large a feature. As well as the red-flowered varieties of dahlias, nicotianas and linums, incude some with bronze foliage such as *Ricinus communis* 'Gibsonii' and some of the cannas or Indian shot. Green foliage plants will help to tone down an otherwise overpowering effect and can include annual ornamental grasses and the burning bush or *Kochia scoparia* (this turns red later in the year).

Yellow border Yellow flowers and foliage create a bright sunny effect which will show up well at dusk. A bed or border of yellow plants will need a dark green background such as an evergreen hedge, otherwise the plants will not show up. There's no need to use all yellow plants: cream flowers could be included together with some plants with grey or silver foliage such as *Cineraria maritima, Onopordum acanthium* and *Verbascum bombyciferum.*

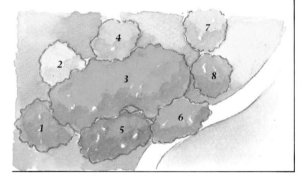

Blue border In a hot summer blue is a refreshing sight, but include some cream or white as well to prevent a 'cold' atmosphere. Don't forget, too, some plants with silver or grey foliage. Some lovely effects can be created by combining pale and dark blue, and even violet flowers.

Pink and silver border Another classic combination, pink and silver, creates a pretty rather than a dramatic effect and this can be charming in a cottage garden. Some good pink-flowered annuals include lavatera varieties, *Cleome spinosa*, *Silene pendula* and *Agrostemma 'Milas'*. Include white flowers, too, such as gypsophila and *Alyssum maritimum (Lobularia maritima)* and silver-foliage plants such as onopordum and *Cineraria maritima*.

Green and white border Green and white is a classic combination, creating a restful, cool atmosphere in the garden. There are several annuals with white flowers, such as gypsophila and alyssum, but fewer with green blooms – the major ones here are *Nicotiana* 'Lime Green' and *Zinnia* 'Envy', and *Euphorbia marginata* is green and white. Include green foliage plants such as the annual ornamental grasses (briza and coix) and silver or grey-leaved subjects like *Cineraria maritima*.

PINK AND SILVER BORDER

1 *Gypsophila elegans*
2 *Agrostema 'Milas'*
3 *Cineraria maritima*
4 *Lavatera 'Loveliness'*
5 *Alyssum maritimum*
6 *Cleome spinosa*
7 *Onopordum acanthium*
8 *Silene pendula*

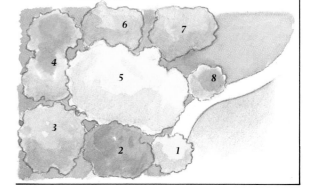

Strong colour Another idea is to use a few strong colours to create impact. You could follow the colour wheel around and have red, purple, blue, deep yellow and orange flowers.

Pastel colours Alternatively combine a few pastel colours, again following the colour wheel: pinks, mauves, pale blues and cream or pale yellow.

The Rainbow Effect

If you want to use many colours in a border then a 'safe' way to arrange them is in a progressive sequence popularly known as the rainbow effect. This prevents any possibility of unpleasant combinations and colour clashing.

A popular way of arranging the colours is to start at one end of the border with flowers in shades of blue; white flowers come next and then pale yellow followed by pink. Then continue on with the stronger colours; scarlet, orange and finally red. This is a good idea for a border of hardy annuals, some of which come in a range of colours that can be difficult to arrange effectively if you are not experienced in colour planning.

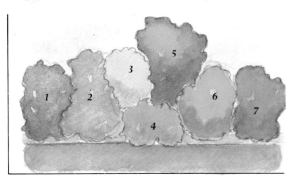

Separating Strong Colours

Another way of playing safe to prevent possible colour clashes when using a wide range of colours in a bed or border is to separate strong colours such as the reds, oranges and bright pinks with white or green flowers. Or by using foliage plants of white, silver, grey or green.

THE RAINBOW EFFECT

1 *Centaurea cyanus*
2 *Gypsophila elegans*
3 *Verbascum bombyciferum*
4 *Helipterum roseum*
5 *Linum grandiflorum rubrum*
6 *Calendula officinalis*
7 *Alonsoa warscewiczii*

Using Multi-Coloured Flowers

Many annuals and biennials are supplied by seedsmen as mixtures of a few or many colours. Some mixtures contain shades of one colour, others a lot of different colours such as reds, yellows and blues. And other annuals and biennials have two or more colours in the one flower, which ar known as bi-coloured flowers. The effects produced from these plants can be either harmonious or contrasting.

So how do we handle plants which come in mixtures? A complete bed of multi-coloured flowers can be very effective. A spring display of mixed wallflowers, pansies, polyanthus and double daisies is extremely lively. Plant each kind in a bold group, patch or drift.

Groups of multi-coloured flowers can also be combined with groups of single colours, again aiming for harmony or contrast.

Mixtures that contain shades of one colour should be treated as single colours for the purposes of colour planning.

It should be borne in mind that using too many multi-coloured flowers can create a fussy or spotty effect in the garden. Generally speaking, it is easier to use single colours when planning colour schemes.

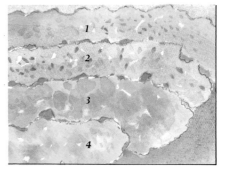

MULTI-COLOURED BED

1 *Wallflower 'Fair Lady Mixed'*
2 *Pansies 'Floral Dance'*
3 *Double daisies*
4 *Polyanthus 'Pacific Giants'*

Planning Tips

Any planting scheme should be planned on paper, taking into account colour, flowering time and height. If colour combinations are to be effective it goes without saying that all of the plants must flower at the same time. But do not stick too rigidly to the general rule of tall at the back, short at the front or you will end up with a border that is far too regimented. So bring the occasional group of tall plants and a few groups of shorter plants towards the centre of the border. In a bed that is viewed from all sides the taller plants should be grouped in the centre.

Prepare a colour sketch of the planting scheme, to show whether the colour combinations work. If they look pleasing to your eye, that's fine. Colour planning is, after all, a personal business. There is no need to go into elaborate detail here so don't worry if you are not much of an artist. Have a go with a box of artist's watercolour paints or with coloured felt-tipped pens.

Planting Schemes

Specific planting schemes using hardy and half-hardy annuals and biennials have many uses in the garden and can be grown in all kinds of places. Those shown here should be treated as starting points for individual imaginations to take over.

Borders

Traditional annuals borders Hardy annuals are traditionally grown in their own border, which makes a highly colourful feature in the summer. The border should ideally be backed by a dark green hedge. A wall or a dark fence would also make a suitable background. If there is a lawn in front of this border the annuals will show up really well.

The traditional annual border is nowhere near as popular today as it was in the past because gardens are now much smaller and there is not the space available to devote a whole bed to one type of plant. However it is an idea that might appeal to owners of brand new gardens because it is a quick and cheap way of providing colour and filling bare ground. Later, it can be turned gradually into a mixed border.

How do we plan an annual border? One way is to arrange the plants in a progressive rainbow sequence, as mentioned earlier. Or the colours could be mixed, taking into account harmony and contrast.

Each variety should be sown in bold informal splashes as it is far more pleasing to have fewer larger groups. So, if you have a small border, choose only a few varieties.

Mixed borders Many gardens today have mixed borders containing all kinds of plants. And this is sensible if you have a small garden. The main framework of a mixed border consists of shrubs, both deciduous and evergreen (a good balance is one-third evergreens to two-thirds deciduous) and, ideally, flowers and foliage will determine the varieties selected.

Among the shrubs are planted herbaceous perennials, bulbs, hardy annuals, half-hardy annuals and biennials. Here, too, the rule stands firm – bold groups or drifts for best effect.

When choosing plants for a mixed border it is important that they associate well with the shrubs – not all plants do so by any means.

With hardy annuals I prefer to use species plants rather than man-made hybrids, some of which are too flamboyant and just do not look right. Hardy annuals are particularly useful for filling any gaps, and there may be quite a few for the first few years.

Suitable hardy annuals for a mixed border are: *Argemone*

mexicana, *Briza maxima, Coix lacryma-jobi, Eschscholzia californica (California Poppy), Euphorbia marginata, Gilia capitata, Glaucium corniculatum, Helipterum roseum (Rhodanthe), Linum grandiflorum* 'Rubrum', *Lupinus texensis, Malcolmia maritima (Virginia Stock), Malope trifida* Grandiflora', *Mentzelia lindleyi (Bartonia aurea), Mirabilis jalapa (Four o'clock Plant), Nemophila menziesii, Phacelia campanularia, Silene pendula* and *Tropaeolum peregrinum (Canary Creeper).*

Half-hardy annuals are only planted in the mixed border when all danger of frost is over. Again they are useful for filling any gaps and should not be excessively flamboyant. I particularly recommend the following: *Ageratum houstonianum,* makes a good edging; *Amaranthus caudatus* (Love Lies Bleeding); *Begonia semperflorens,* looks good planted in drifts at the front of the border; *Cleome spinosa; Dahlia variabilis,* preferably in single colours, the dwarf ones being ideal for the front of the border; *Heliotropium arborescens (Heliotrope); Lobelia erinus,* which looks lovely planted in bold informal drifts at the front; *Nicotiana alata (Ornamental Tobacco),* particularly the variety 'Lime Green', *Ricinus communis,* for foliage effect; *Verbena x hybrida,* planted in drifts at the front; and *Zea mays,* for foliage effect.

Many hardy biennials are suitable for the mixed border including double daisies or *Bellis perennis,* which can be used

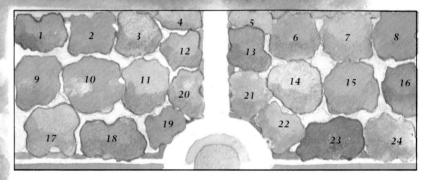

TRADITIONAL ANNUAL BORDER

1 Calendula officinalis	13 Godetia grandiflora
2 Chrysanthemum carinatum	14 Anchusa capensis 'Blue Bird'
3 Salvia horminum	15 Delphinium consolida
4 Centaurea cyanus 'Blue Diadem'	16 Reseda odorata 'Red Monarch'
5 Gypsophila elegans	17 Dianthus chinensis
6 Lavatera trimestris 'Silver Cup'	18 Nemophila menziesii
7 Helianthus annuus	19 Eschscholzia californica
8 Clarkia elegans	20 Phacelia campanularia
9 Lupinus texensis	21 Silene pendula
10 Papaver nudicaule	22 Malcolmia maritima
11 Nigella damascena 'Miss Jekyll'	23 Iberis umbellata
12 Mentzelia lindleyi	24 Linum grandiflorum 'Rubrum'

as edging or planted in bold drifts at the front; *Campanula medium* or Canterbury bells; sweet williams or *Dianthus barbatus;* foxgloves or *Digitalis purpurea,* particularly the 'Excelsior Strain', for the back of the border; *Lunaria annua* or honesty; *Myosotis sylvatica* planted in drifts; *Onopordum acanthium,* the Scotch thistle grown for its striking foliage and which should be planted at the back of the border; polyanthus or *Primula polyantha* which can be drifted among shrubs; and pansies or varieties of *Viola x wittrockiana* which should again be planted in bold drifts at the front – blue or yellow shades look particularly effective.

To create 'themes' in the mixed border, group plants by their flowering seasons. For example for a spring display plant spring-flowering biennials such as polyanthus, honesty and forget-me-nots around spring-flowering shrubs such as forsythia.

Summer-flowering plants such as dahlias and nicotiana can be grouped around summer-flowering shrubs and are also particularly effective combined with coloured-foliage shrubs such as purple cotinus or berberis or golden philadelphus.

Foxgloves makes marvellous companions for the early summer flowering philadelphus or mock orange.

COTTAGE GARDEN BORDER

1 *Althaea rosea 'Summer Carnival'*
2 *Sweet pea*
3 *Dianthus barbatus*
4 *Campanula medium*
4 *Digitalis 'Excelsior'*
6 *Molucella laevis*
7 *Malcolmia maritima*
8 *Lunaria annua*
9 *Dianthus chinensis*
10 *Shrubs*

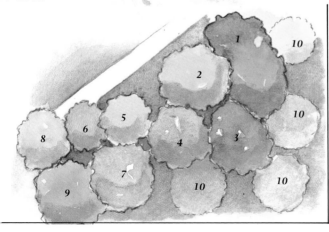

The cottage-garden border This is essentially a traditional English country style of gardening. Small cottage gardens of the past (belonging mainly to those who worked on the land) were a glorious mixture of all kinds of plants, including vegetables and fruits, and there was no thought at all given to planning or colour schemes.

This style of gardening is becoming popular again, not only with those who own cottages in the country but also with city and town dwellers who are finding that the cottage-garden style does not look out of place in the confined plots of modern town houses.

It is appropriate to use old-fashioned hardy annuals and biennials in a cottage-style garden and the following can be recommended:

Althaea rosea (Hollyhocks), *Calendula officinalis* (Marigolds), *Campanula medium* (Canterbury Bells), *Centaurea cyanus* (Cornflowers), *Cheiranthus cheiri* (Wallflowers), *Delphinium consolida* (Larkspurs), *Dianthus barbatus* (Sweet Williams), *Dianthus chinensis*, *Digitalis purpurea* (Foxgloves), *Iberis umbellata* (Candytufts), *Lathyrus odoratus* (Sweet Peas), *Lunaria annua* (Honesty), *Malcolmia maritima* (Virginia Stocks), *Matthiola incana* (Stocks), *Molucella laevis* (Bells of Ireland), *Myosotis sylvatica* (Forget-me-nots), *Nigella damascena* (Love in a Mist), *Reseda odorata* (Mignonette), *Scabiosa atropurpurea* (Scabious), *Tropaeolum majus* (Nasturtiums), *Verbascum bombyciferum* and *Viola x wittrockiana* (Pansies), particularly the small-flowered viola types.

Beds

Sub-tropical bedding This is a very popular form of summer bedding using half-hardy annuals – mainly foliage kinds – but a few flowering types too. The idea is to create a sub-tropical atmosphere – for instance, around a patio. Plants should be arranged informally in bold groups. Foliage kinds include *Ricinus communis*, *Canna x generalis*, *Amaranthus tricolor* varieties and *Coleus blumei*. For a sub-tropical scheme, choose exotic-looking flowers such as *Begonia semperflorens*, *Impatiens wallerana* (Busy Lizzie), *Amaranthus caudatus* (Love lies Bleeding) and *Celosia plumosa* (Prince of Wales' Feathers).

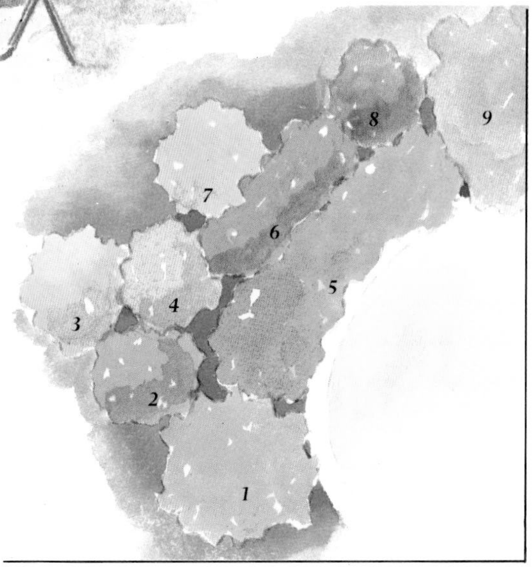

SUB-TROPICAL BED

1 *Begonia semperflorens*
2 *Amaranthus caudatus*
3 *Celosia plumosa*
4 *Amaranthus tricolor 'Illumination'*
5 *Begonia semperflorens*
6 *Impatiens wallerana*
7 *Canna x generalis*
8 *Ricinus communis 'Impala'*
9 *Coleus blumei*

Summer bedding schemes The most popular use of half-hardy annuals is in summer bedding schemes. The plants are mass planted in formal beds that are often sited close to the house and/or patio. The purpose here is to provide a mass of bright colour.

There is a tried and tested way of arranging the plants. First there is the main carpet of plants which can cover most or all of the bed. This can consist of one type of plant or several intermixed and normally low growing. For example you could have a carpet of *Begonia semperflorens*; a mix of zonal or bedding geraniums and petunias; scarlet salvias; or marigolds combined with *Verbena venosa*.

Then there is an edging to the carpet, again using a low-growing subject that contrasts with the main carpet. To be effective an edging needs to be reasonably wide – about 30cm (12in). Typical edging plants are ageratum, *Alyssum maritimum*, lobelia and golden pyrethrum.

A carpet of plants with strongly coloured flowers (such as scarlet salvias or bedding geraniums) needs relieving in some way otherwise the effect can be overpowering, so we plant at

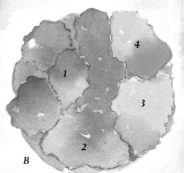

HALF-HARDY ANNUAL BEDS

A1 *Nicotiana 'Lime Green'*
  2 *Cineraria maritima*
  3 *Salvia splendens*
  4 *Alyssum maritimum*

B1 *Canna x generalis*
  2 *Heliotrope 'Marine'*
  3 *Verbena venosa*
  4 *African Marigold 'Inca Yellow'*

random within the carpet some plants which act as a foil. These are taller than the carpet and are popularly known as dot plants. Suitable subjects include the silver-leaved *Cineraria maritima* and heliotrope.

So far we do not have much height so we can include some tall plants, perhaps in the centre of the bed or give a random effect of structure to the entire bed. The ornamental maize, *Zea mays,* is especially useful and so too is the castor oil plant or *Ricinus communis.* Varieties of *Canna x generalis* are highly recommended for their bold foliage. Other tall plants include some of the nicotianas, African marigolds and standard plants (grown like small trees) or zonal geraniums and heliotrope.

The possible combinations of plants for summer bedding are virtually limitless but the accompanying illustrations give a few examples which hopefully will get you started.

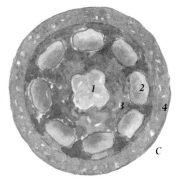

HALF-HARDY ANNUAL BEDS

C1 *Zea mays 'Gigantea Quadricolor'*
 2 *Heliotrope 'Marine'*
 3 *Begonia semperflorens*
 4 *Ageratum*

D1 *Ricinus communis 'Gibsonii'*
 2 *Pelargonium 'Orange Orbit'*
 3 *Petunias*

Spring bedding schemes Here we use hardy biennials which are mass planted in a similar way to summer bedding schemes. Again they are frequently grown in formal beds around the house or patio but the display is provided in the spring. Spring bedding plants are planted in the autumn as soon as the summer bedding plants have been cleared.

Again we plant a main carpet of plants which may be wallflowers, forget-me-nots, polyanthus or double daisies. Often we interplant with tulips which grow through the carpet and flower above it. The beds can be edged if desired with a contrasting edging plant – double daisies and forget-me-nots are often used for this purpose.

Alternatively, you could get away from these traditional arrangements and have several large informal groups or drifts of different plants such as wallflowers, polyanthus and winter-flowering pansies (which bloom also in spring).

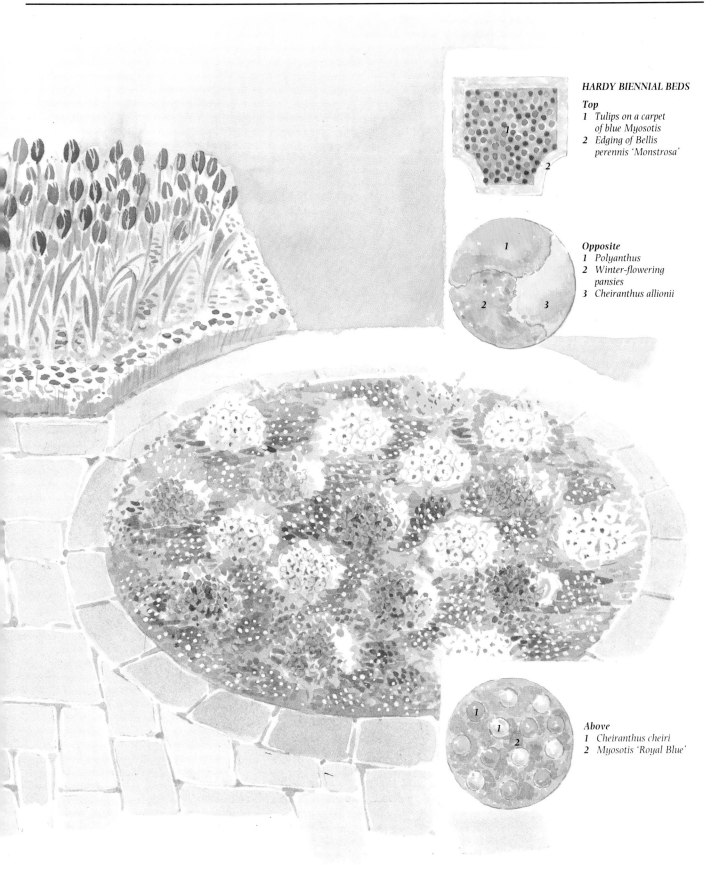

HARDY BIENNIAL BEDS

Top
1 Tulips on a carpet of blue Myosotis
2 Edging of Bellis perennis 'Monstrosa'

Opposite
1 Polyanthus
2 Winter-flowering pansies
3 Cheiranthus allionii

Above
1 Cheiranthus cheiri
2 Myosotis 'Royal Blue'

Containers

Growing colourful plants in ornamental containers, such as tubs and urns on patios and terraces, is very popular. Window boxes are also widely used to provide colour on a higher level. Half-hardy annuals are used for the summer display and hardy biennials for spring colour.

The usual way of arranging plants in tubs, etc, is to have tallish plants such as zonal geraniums in the centre and to plant trailing kinds such as *Verbena x hybrida*, trailing lobelia or petunias around the edge. With window boxes you can aim for a triangular shape by planting tallish plants in the middle and grading down to each end with shorter plants. Trailers can be planted to hang over the front and ends.

Some popular half-hardy annuals for containers are *Ageratum houstonianum, Begonia semperflorens, Begonia tuberosa* (Tuberous Begonia), *Gazania x hybrida, Heliotropium arborescens* (Heliotrope), *Impatiens wallerana* (Busy Lizzie), *Lobelia erinus, Mimulus x hybridus, Nicotiana alata* (dwarf varieties), *Pelargonium x hortorum* (Zonal Geranium), *Petunia x hybrida, Salvia splendens, Cineraria Maritina* (Silver-leaved Cineraria), *Tagetes patula* (French Marigold), *Tagetes tenuifolia* and *Verbena x hybrida*.

Hardy biennials which grow well in containers include *Bellis perennis* (Double Daisy), *Cheiranthus cheiri* (Wallflowers), *Cheiranthus allionii* (Siberian Wallflower), *Myosotis sylvatica* (Forget-me-not), *Primula polyantha* (Polyanthus) and winter-flowering pansies or *Viola x wittrockiana*. Spring-flowering bulbs such as tulips (particularly dwarf varieties) and hyacinths can be planted among these.

URN

1 *Cineraria maritima*
2 *Petunias*

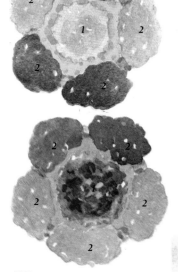

TUB

1 *Pelargonium x hortorum*
2 *Verbena x hybrida*

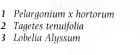

1 *Pelargonium x hortorum*
2 *Tagetes tenuifolia*
3 *Lobelia Alyssum*

SHADE

1 *Cineraria maritima*
2 *Impatiens wallerana*

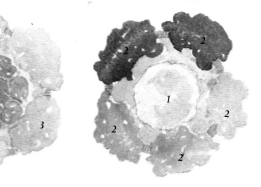

Hanging Baskets

Hanging baskets are very popular for providing colour on a higher level. They can be hung on the walls of the house, particularly in the area of a patio, on garage and garden walls, and on pergolas. They do need constant care and watering to be successful, however.

For the best effect – a complete ball of colour – wire baskets are best, because plants can be inserted through the wires in the sides as well as in the top. With solid-sided baskets it is possible to plant only in the top.

Half-hardy annuals are used for baskets, and the way to arrange them is to have bushy plants in the centre to give height, some shorter plants around these if there is sufficient space, and trailing kinds around the edge and also planted through the wires.

For a sunny aspect, a basket with a red-orange zonal geranium at the centre surrounded with dwarf orange *Tagetes tenuifolia* and trailing lobelia mixed with white alyssum can make a dramatic feature; while for a position in shade try a basket of impatiens in mixed colours with a centrepiece of silvery *Cineraria maritima*.

Other trailing plants for baskets include ageratum, pendulous tuberous begonias, petunias and trailing varieties of verbena. More upright plants for the centre include tuberous and fibrous-rooted begonias, coleus, heliotrope, French marigolds and mimulus.

Rock Gardens and Paved Areas

Some of the small hardy annuals are ideal for adding colour to a rock garden during the summer, by which time most alpines have finished flowering. Small annuals can also be sown in gaps in paving, particularly in the crazy paving (random-stone paving) which is often a feature of cottage gardens.

Some recommended annuals are *Convolvulus tricolor*, *Dianthus chinensis*, *Eschscholzia californica* (Californian Poppy), *Iberis umbellata* (Candytuft), *Ionopsidium acaule*, *Linaria maroccana*, *Malcolmia maritima* (Virginia Stock), *Nemophila menziesii*, *Phacelia campanularia* and *Viola x wittrockiana* (viola types).

Try also the following half-hardy annuals, planting them out when danger of frost is over: *Dimorphotheca aurantiaca* (*Star of the Beldt*), *Gazania x hybrida*, *Lobelia erinus*, *Nemesia strumosa*, *Phlox drummondii*, *Portulaca grandiflora* and *Tagetes tenuifolia*.

Specimen Plants

Sometimes we need a focal point in the garden to lead the eye to a particular part – for instance, at the end of a lawn or in a corner of the garden. Tall bold plants are called for here, ideally planted in a group of maximum impact. Several of the plants described in this book are suitable for creating focal points, and use light-coloured plants such as onopordum and verbascum to create a sense of distance. And we would recommend: *Althaea rosea* (Hollyhock), *Digitalis purpurea* (Foxglove), *Helianthus annuus* (Sunflower), *Onopordum acanthium*, *Ricinus communis*, *Verbascum bombyciferum* and *Zea mays*.

Walls and Fences

There are several climbers featured in the book which are ideal for clothing walls and fences. Remember, though, that climbing annuals can also be grown up trelliswork and pillars. They can also be allowed to scramble over large shrubs or cascade down banks.

The following climbers are worth considering: *Cobaea scandens*, *Cucurbita pepo ovifera* (Ornamental Gourds), *Ipomoea tricolor* (Convolvulus), *Lathyrus odoratus* (Sweet Pea), *Thunbergia alata*, *Tropaeolum majus* (Nasturtium) (some varieties climb) and *Tropaeolum peregrinum* (Canary Creeper).

Wild Areas

Many people are devoting areas of their garden to wild flowers. Growing wild meadow flowers in grass has the advantage that the grass needs cutting only once a year so being labour-saving as well as a conservation area. A long-grass area would be suitable for a bank; or a carefully selected part of the lawn could be devoted to wild flowers, creating a nice contrast between mown and long grass. But don't plan a wild area too close to cultivated beds – seeding would be a great arrogance.

There are also wild flowers suitable for woodland conditions, so anyone with an area of woodland could devote part of it to native plants.

Seedsmen on both sides of the Atlantic supply seeds of native wild flowers, both separate and in mixtures suited to different purposes. It is also possible to buy mixtures of wild meadow flowers and grass seeds, so that you can sow both in one operation. Some wild flowers are annuals and will seed themselves every year, while others are perennial.

The best time to cut a flower meadow is in late summer or early autumn, once the wild flowers have finished blooming and the seeds have set.

Catalogue of Annuals and Biennials

This catalogue of annuals and biennials has been arranged by the predominant colour of the flowers, and this is to help you plan colour schemes for different effects in different parts of the garden. The plant descriptions and special attributes are followed by hints on cultivation and propagation.

KEY TO SYMBOLS

Spread: This is the maximum width of the plant under ideal growing conditions and is also a guide to planting or thinning distances.

Height: The maximum height under ideal growing conditions.

HA   Hardy Annual

HHA   Half-Hardy Annual

HB   Hardy Biennial

☀	Full sun
☀	Partial shade
✸	Full shade
S	Scented
	Climber
	Trailer
	Climber/Trailer
	Interesting foliage
✂	Suitable for cut flowers
	Ideal for planting singly
	Ideal for planting in groups

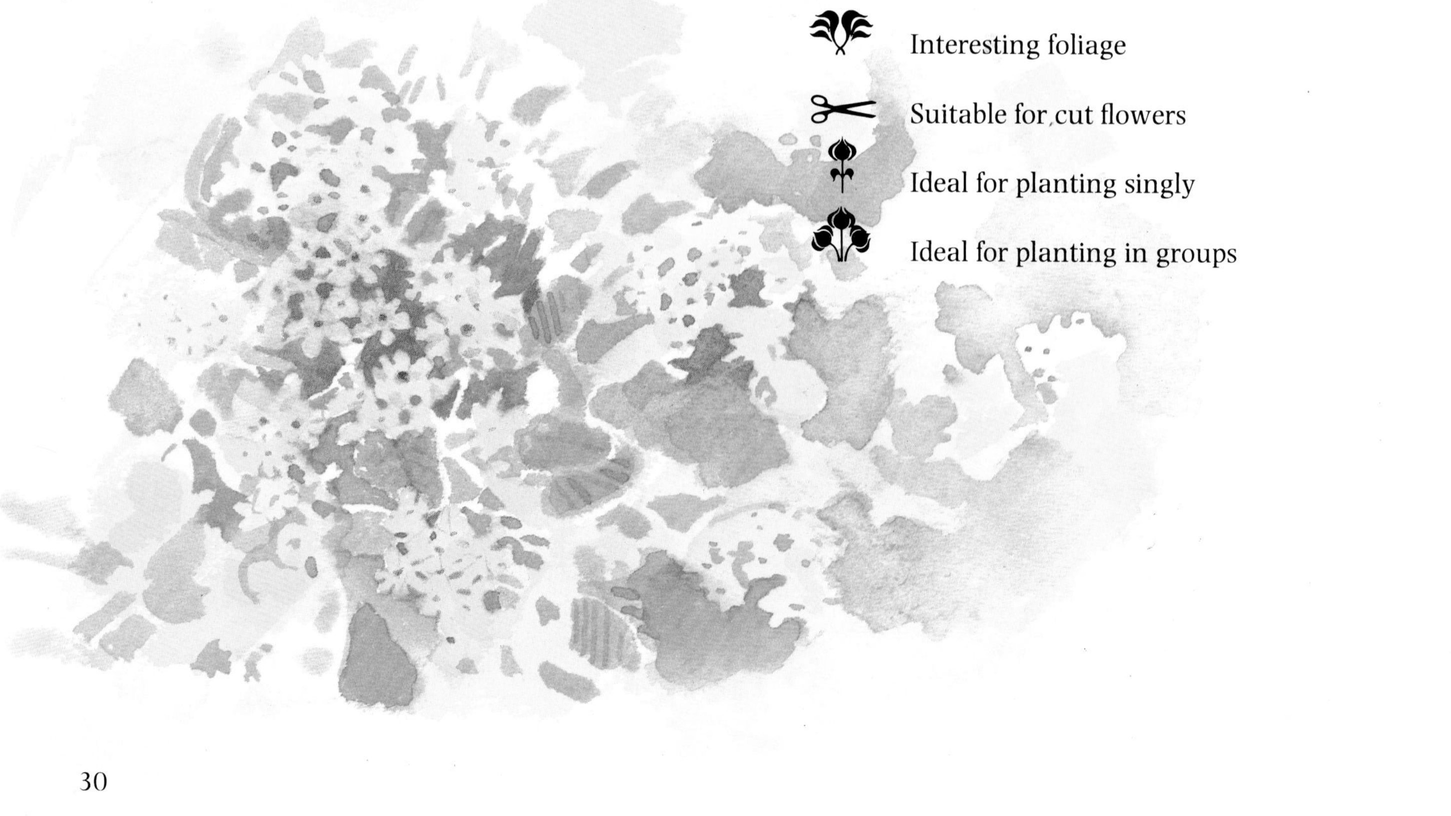

Briza maxima
Greater Quaking Grass

Spread 15–20cm (6–8in)
Height 60cm (24in)

HA

Coix lacryma-jobi
Job's Tears

Spread 20cm (8in)
Height 90cm (36in)

HHA

The Greater Quaking Grass has attractive bright green foliage and silvery brownish flowers, making an ideal foil for strongly coloured flowers. One of the best of the annual grasses, it may be dried and used for winter decoration if cut before the seeds heads ripen.

CULTIVATION
A position in full sun with well-drained soil will suit this grass. Make sure the soil is not too rich.

PROPAGATION
Sow seeds in early to mid-spring where the plants are to grow and thin out seedlings before they become overcrowded.

This grass has broad medium-green leaves in tufts and greyish green seeds in clusters on arching stems. The main attraction is the seed heads which unfortunately are not suitable for cutting and drying. Job's Tears makes a good foil for brightly coloured flowers and looks particulary at home in a cottage garden.

CULTIVATION
This grass must have full sun and a very well-drained soil. It will appreciate plenty of organic matter in the soil such as garden compost or peat.

PROPAGATION
Sow seeds during late winter/early spring in warmth, indoors or in a greenhouse. Prick out seedlings into 7.5cm (3in) pots and plant out when danger of frost is over. Alternatively sow outdoors in mid-spring.

Euphorbia marginata
Snow on the Mountain

Spread 30cm (12in)
Height 60cm (24in)   **HA**

Kochia scoparia 'Trichophylla'
Burning Bush

Spread 60cm (24in)
Height 90cm (36in)   **HHA**

This annual has a bushy habit of growth and white-edged bright green foliage bracts at the top of the plant. The flowers which appear in summer are insignificant. Snow on the Mountain is popular for cutting for use in flower arrangements. When cut it exudes a white sap which can be stopped by dipping the bases of the stems in hot water.

It is an especially useful annual for filling gaps in shrub borders and would also look at home in a cottage garden. It is indispensable for green and white planting schemes. There is a variety called 'White Icicle' which is faster growing than the species.

CULTIVATION
Any well-drained soil is suitable, in full sun or partial shade. In dry poor soils the foliage colour is much better.

PROPAGATION
Best treated as a half hardy annual, but also can be sown in early to mid-spring where the plants are to grow and thinning out seedlings before they become overcrowded.

For many years the Burning Bush has been popular for summer bedding schemes in which it is often used as a dot plant. It forms a conifer-like bush of feathery foliage, which at first is light green but gradually changes to deep red. There is another variety named 'Childsii' which has a neater habit and is more compact than 'Trichophylla', but does not go red in the autumn.

CULTIVATION
The ideal situation is full sun with a light well drained soil, but plants will grow in any kind of soil. If the garden is prone to wind it may be necessary to provide supports for the plants: a thin bamboo cane for each one will be sufficient, tying in with soft garden string or raffia.

PROPAGATION
Sow the seeds in heat, in a greenhouse or indoors in early spring, and prick out the seedlings individually into 7.5cm (3in) pots. Plant out when danger of frost is over. Seeds may also be sown outdoors in mid-spring.

Molucella laevis
Bells of Ireland

Spread 20cm (8in)
Height 60cm (24in)

HHA

This is a favourite cottage-garden annual and the flowers are often dried for use in winter flower arrangements. It has roundish leaves which are pale green and in summer it sends up flower spikes carrying small white blooms, each surrounded by a large light green leaf-like calyx shaped like a shell. An excellent annual for filling gaps in a shrub or mixed border and for 'cool' green and white planting schemes.

CULTIVATION
Grow in any ordinary garden soil but ideally in a light well-drained one well supplied with organic matter and fertilizer. Choose a site in full sun for best results.

PROPAGATION
Sow seeds in early spring, in a greenhouse or indoors, providing warmth for germination. Seedlings can be pricked out into trays or individual 7.5cm (3in) pots. Harden off and plant out when danger of frost is over. Alternatively sow outdoors in mid-spring where the plants are to flower.

Zea mays
Ornamental Maize

Spread 60cm (24in)
Height 1–1.8m (3–6ft)

HHA

Ornamental Maize is often used to give height and contrast in summer bedding schemes. It can also be used in sub-tropical bedding schemes, in shrub or mixed borders or grown as a specimen plant to act as a focal point in the garden. It has large grassy foliage and large seed heads known as cobs. There are several varieties such as 'Gigantea Quadricolor' with leaves variegated in white, pink and light yellow; 'Japonica Multicolor' whose cobs contain red, yellow, orange and blue seeds; and 'Strawberry Corn' with strawberry shaped red cobs.

CULTIVATION
Full sun is essential together with soil that has been well-supplied with organic matter and fertilizer. Plenty of water is needed in summer.

PROPAGATION
Sow seeds in warmth under glass or indoors in mid-spring, one per 7.5cm (3in) pot. Plant out when danger of frost is over. Alternatively sow outdoors in late spring.

Alyssum maritimum (Lobularia maritima)
Sweet Alyssum

Spread 20–30cm (8–12in)
Height 7.5–15cm (3–6in)

HA

Alyssum is in the top-ten list of summer bedding plants and rightly so because it is very easily propagated and grown and flowers profusely for months on end.

It forms a hummocky mat of growth and when in full flower the foliage is barely visible. The individual flowers are tiny but are carried in clustered heads.

The traditional colour of Sweet Alyssum is white, and popular varieties in this colour include 'Little Dorrit', with an upright habit of growth and 'Carpet of Snow', a low-growing spreading variety with masses of pure white blooms.

There are varieties with flowers in other colours and these are becoming almost as popular as the white varieties. Particularly recommended are 'Rosie O'Day' in a most attractive clear rose-pink; 'Wonderland', with beautiful rich rose-red flowers and a sweet scent, borne on compact plants; and 'Oriental Night' with intense violet-purple flowers on compact plants with a spread of 20cm (8in).

Sweet Alyssum can be used in many ways for summer colour. Probably the most popular use is as edging to beds or borders, particularly if the planting consists of strongly coloured plants such as scarlet salvias or pelargoniums. It looks good planted in a wide band – at least 30cm (12in) – rather than in a thin strip.

Drifts of white alyssum look superb among shrubs in a mixed or shrub border and it *must* be included in any green and white planting scheme. It can also be grown on a rock garden to provide colour when the spring-flowering alpines have finished their display.

Sweet Alyssum is often used with other plants, such as lobelia and petunias, in ornamental containers such as hanging baskets, window boxes, tubs and urns: it is generally planted at the edges so that it cascades over the sides of the containers. It can be planted through the wires of hanging baskets, perhaps alternatively with blue lobelia. Alyssum will look perfectly at home in a cottage-garden border.

CULTIVATION
Alyssum will grow in any ordinary well-drained soil and best results are achieved in full sun. Shade for a small part of the day would be acceptable, though. Regularly remove dead flower heads with a pair of florists' scissors.

PROPAGATION
Sow seeds under glass or indoors in late winter/early spring and germinate in gentle heat. Prick out seedlings into trays, harden off and plant out in mid- or late spring. Alternatively sow outdoors in mid-spring where the plant are to flower.

Cineraria maritima
Silver-leaved Cineraria

Spread 30cm (12in)
Height 60cm (24in)

HHA

Although perennial this popular summer bedding plant is generally treated as a half-hardy annual. It will only survive mild winters out of doors. It has lobed and deeply cut leaves which are silvery grey, and the plant makes an excellent foil for bedding plants with strongly coloured flowers, such as scarlet pelargoniums and salvias. Use it as a dot plant in summer bedding schemes; also in containers such as tubs and window boxes. An excellent plant for a pink and silver planting scheme. Good varieties include 'Cirrus' and 'Silver Dust'.

The Silver-leaved Cineraria is an excellent temporary plant, too, for the mixed border, being ideal for filling gaps at the front of the border, especially if it can be combined with brightly coloured flowers or shrubs. It can also be recommended for edging beds of roses, as the silver foliage is a marvellous foil for highly coloured rose blooms.

There is no need to throw plants away at the end of the season – lift and pot them into suitable-size pots and grow as pot plants in a cool or slightly heated greenhouse. Or even take them into a cool room indoors where the foliage can be enjoyed over the winter.

CULTIVATION
Any ordinary well-drained soil is suitable and best growth is achieved in full sun, although the plant will not mind shade for part of the day. Cut off any flowers produced as they do not enhance the plants.

PROPAGATION
Sow seeds under glass or indoors in late winter/early spring and provide warmth for germination. Prick out seedlings into trays and plant out when the danger of frost is over. Alternatively, prick out individually into small pots.

Gypsophila elegans
Baby's Breath

Spread 30cm (12in)
Height 60cm (24in)

HA

This annual is an excellent foil for plants with strong coloured flowers and is good for separating strong or clashing colours. It is highly recommended for cutting and is often arranged with sweet peas. It looks at home in a shrub or mixed border and should be included in every green and white planting scheme.

Good varieties are 'Monarch Strain' and 'Giant White'.

CULTIVATION
Needs a well-drained soil but any type is suitable and it is particularly good on chalky soils. Provide a position in full sun for best results. Use twiggy sticks to support the thin stems.

PROPAGATION
Sow seeds in their flowering positions in early to mid-spring and thin out seedlings. Can also be sown in early autumn when flowering will be earlier the following year.

Matricaria eximea (Chrysanthemum parthenium)
Feverfew

Spread 20–45cm (8–18in)
Height 20–45cm (8–18in)

HA  S

Strictly speaking this is a short-lived perennial but it is generally treated as a hardy annual and discarded at the end of its flowering season. It's a bushy plant with aromatic foliage and in summer produces masses of button-like flowers. There are several varieties such as 'Snow Dwarf' ('White Stars') with double white flowers; 'Snowball', also white; and the golden-yellow 'Golden Ball'.

Feverfew is particularly useful for edging beds and borders, preferably in a wide band. It would also look good on a rock garden and is ideal for the edges of ornamental containers such as window boxes and tubs.

CULTIVATION
Any well-drained soil in full sun. Regularly remove dead flowers to encourage more to follow.

PROPAGATION
Generally raised under glass in early spring to get earlier flowers, but can also be sown outdoors in mid-spring where it is to flower.

Onopordum acanthium
Scotch Thistle

Spread 60cm (24in)
Height 1.8m (6ft)

HB

This is a really bold plant with branching winged stems and huge silvery-grey hairy leaves. During the summer the plant produces heads of purple thistle flowers. It's an extremely prickly plant so do not plant it where you are liable to brush by it!

The Scotch Thistle makes a superb specimen plant to act as a focal point in the garden. It can also be grown in a shrub or mixed border. It seeds itself so you may well find seedlings appearing around the parent plants.

CULTIVATION
Growth will be vigorous in a rich soil. Drainage must be good and a position which receives plenty of sun is needed. To prevent self-seeding remove dead flower heads. Protect plants from slugs.

PROPAGATION
Sow seeds in late spring where the plants are to grow and flower. Alternatively, sow under glass in early or mid-spring, one seed per small pot, and plant out before the seedlings become pot-bound.

The plants will flower the following year, after which they die.

Reseda odorata
Mignonette

Spread 30cm (12in)
Height 30–60cm (12–24in)

HA

A lovely old-fashioned annual with scented flowers, often grown in cottage gardens. It also looks at home in shrubberies or mixed borders and, of course, in annual borders. The blooms are excellent for cutting and arranging indoors. In the garden they attract bees.

The plant has an upright branching habit of growth and in summer bears off-white flowers. There are several varieties such as 'Fragrant Beauty', particularly well scented; 'Machet' with red-flushed blooms; and 'Red Monarch' which has red flowers.

CULTIVATION
An excellent annual for chalky or limy soils, although these conditions are not essential. Good drainage is, though. Be fairly generous with the fertilizer. Regularly remove dead flower heads to encourage more blooms to follow.

PROPAGATION
So seeds in early to mid-spring where the plants are to flower and thin out the resultant seedlings before they become overcrowded. Or sow under glass in early spring and plant out before plants become overcrowded in their trays. They will flower earlier. Can also be sown in early autumn to overwinter outdoors – again plants will flower earlier.

Verbascum bombyciferum (V. 'Broussa') _____
Mullein

Spread 60cm (24in)
Height 1.2–1.8m (4–6ft)

HB

Argemone mexicana _____
Prickly Poppy

Spread 30cm (12in)
Height 60cm (24in)

HA **S**

This is a stately plant with silver hairy leaves and branching stems carrying pale yellow flowers. The flowering period is early to mid-summer.

This Mullein makes a superb specimen plant to act as a focal point in a garden. Alternatively use it at the back of a shrubbery or mixed border.

CULTIVATION
Any ordinary well-drained soil is suitable plus a position in full sun. Staking may be necessary in windy gardens, using a stout bamboo cane for each plant. Cut off the flower spikes when the blooms have faded.

PROPAGATION
Sow seeds in mid-spring and germinate in a cold frame. Prick out into nursery rows and plant in flowering positions in early autumn. Alternatively, plant direct into final positions.

This is an unusual annual and is certainly not found in all seed catalogues, but nevertheless it is easily grown and well worth garden space. The prickly deeply cut leaves are greyish green and attractively marked with white. Flowering starts in early summer and the poppy-like blooms are mainly yellow although sometimes orangy and are scented.

This is a suitable subject for a shubbery, or an annual or mixed border and is best sown in a bold group for maximum impact.

CULTIVATION
This annual revels in a light, dry, sandy soil and full sun, so plant it in those difficult 'hot spots'. Although the stems are somewhat sprawling and succulent the plants should not be provided with supports. Regular removal of dead flowers will encourage more blooms to follow.

PROPAGATION
Sow under glass or indoors during early spring, transplant seedlings into small pots, harden and plant out in late spring. Alternatively sow in the open during mid-spring where the plants are to flower.

Calceolaria integrifolia (C. rugosa)
Slipperwort, Bedding Calceolaria

Spread 30cm (12in)
Height 45–60cm (18–24in)

HHA

Coreopsis tinctoria
Tickseed

Spread 15–20cm (6–8in)
Height 30–90cm (12–36in)

HA

This is one of the bedding calceolarias and strictly speaking is a half-hardy perennial, but plants are generally discarded at the end of the flowering season. It is a bushy plant with a long succession of bright yellow pouched flowers. A popular variety, easily raised from seed, is 'Sunshine'. Also worth growing is 'Golden Bunch' (a *C. rugosa* × *C. herbeo-hybrida* variety).

An attractive annual for summer bedding, containers or rock garden.

CULTIVATION
A light well-drained soil is best plus a sunny sheltered position.

PROPAGATION
Sow seeds in early spring under glass or indoors and germinate in gentle warmth (15°C/60°F). Do not cover seeds with compost. Transplant seedlings into trays; eventually harden and plant out when the danger of frost is over.

This annual has a long succession of daisy-like flowers which are suitable for cutting and arranging indoors. The species has bright yellow flowers but mixtures are also offered with blooms in various shades. Popular are dwarf mixtures which grow to about 30cm (12in) in height. Grow Tickseed in an annual border or sow bold groups in a mixed border.

CULTIVATION
The ideal soil is light, well drained and reasonably fertile. Plenty of sun is needed for sturdy growth and flowering. Twiggy sticks will be needed to support tall plants. Remove dead flower heads to encourage more blooms to follow.

PROPAGATION
Sow seeds where the plants are to flower during early to mid-spring and thin out the seedlings before they become overcrowded, or sow in early autumn to overwinter under cloches for earlier flowers.

Helianthus annuus
Sunflower

Spread 30–45cm (12–18in)
Height 1–3m (3–10ft)

HA

Although the Sunflower is often considered a 'fun plant' and is popular with children on account of its height and huge flowers, it does, nevertheless, make a fine show at the back of a border. The blooms are like massive daisies. The main colour is yellow but mixtures are also offered with flowers in several colours. Most popular are varieties such as 'Giant Single' and 'Sunburst Mixed'. Also worth growing is *H. cucumerifolius* 'Bouquet Mixed'.

Unfortunately in Britain Sunflowers can be disappointing if the summer is wet – as it often is. The blooms appear in late summer and autumn, at which time the air can also be very damp. In wet or damp conditions the blooms may become infected by the fungal disease botrytis or grey mould, which reduces them to a soggy mess. The blooms become covered with grey fluffy fungus. There is really not a great deal one can do about this, except perhaps to spray the plants with systemic fungicide such as benomyl.

It is interesting to note that some farmers in Britain are trying to grow Sunflowers for the seeds, the oil of which is used in the manufacture of margerine. So in the future, if the trials prove successful, we may see vast fields of sunflowers in the countryside!

CULTIVATION
Plenty of sun is needed for sturdy growth and flowering, plus well-drained soil. The tall varieties will need the support of thick bamboo canes, tying in the stems with soft garden string. Remove dead flower heads to prevent self-seeding.

PROPAGATION
Sow seeds where the plants are to flower, in early or mid-spring. Place two or three seeds at each position and thin out the resultant seedlings to leave the strongest one.

Hunnemannia fumariifolia
Mexican Tulip Poppy

Spread 20cm (8in)
Height 60–90cm (24–36in)

HHA

Mentzelia lindleyi (Bartonia aurea)
Blazing Stars

Spread 15–20cm (6–8in)
Height 45cm (18in)

HA

A rather unusual annual but a most attractive one with its brilliant yellow poppy flowers in summer and lacy bluish green foliage. The flowers last well in water so are suitable for cutting. It is best to seal the ends of the stems in a flame before arranging in vases. There is a variety named 'Sunlite' which has semi-double flowers.

Grow the Mexican Tulip Poppy in an annual, mixed or shrub border in a bold group for best effect.

CULTIVATION
A hot dry spot is ideal for this annual. Remove dead flowers. A few small twiggy sticks may be needed for support.

PROPAGATION
Seeds are sown under glass or indoors in early spring, transplanting the seedlings to individual small pots. Harden and plant out when danger of frost is over. Alternatively sow the seeds in the open during mid-spring where the plants are to flower.

This is a popular hardy annual, bushy in habit, with succulent stems, coarsely toothed green foliage and shiny deep yellow cup-shaped flowers each with a central prominent tuft of stamens. The flowering period is early to mid-summer.

Blazing Stars can be most effective in mixed borders, annual borders, in cottage gardens and even on a largish rock garden.

CULTIVATION
A hot dry situation suits this annual and it will even succeed in an exposed windy garden, when it may need a few short twiggy sticks for support.

PROPAGATION
Seeds are sown where the plants are to flower, in early to mid-spring. Thin out the seedlings before they become overcrowded, but do this carefully to avoid damaging the soft succulent seedlings which are to remain.

Pyrethrum parthenium (Chrysanthemum parthenium)
Golden Feather

Spread 20cm (8in)
Height 25cm (10in)

HA

Rudbeckia hirta
Black-eyed Susan

Spread 30–45cm (12–18in)
Height 45–60cm (18–24in)

HHA

Golden Feather is a popular edging plant for summer bedding schemes and has bright yellow foliage which is finely cut. Flowers can be cut off before they open if you feel they detract from the beauty of the plants.

This annual (or strictly speaking, short-lived perennial) can also be grown in containers such as tubs and window boxes, planting it at the edges. Also use it to fill gaps on a rock garden and plant it in gaps in paving.

There are several varieties available such as 'Golden Fleece' and 'Golden Moss'.

CULTIVATION
Any well-drained soil is suitable plus full sun or partial shade. Too much shade will result in loss of leaf colour. If you wish, leave the plants in the ground at the end of the season – they may well overwinter successfully.

PROPAGATION
Sow seeds in early spring under glass or indoors, transplant the seedlings to trays and plant out in late spring. Can be sown out of doors if desired in mid- to late spring but this is not the normal practice.

Although this is a short-lived perennial it is grown as a half-hardy annual. The large yellow black-eyed daisy flowers are extremely showy and excellent for cutting and arranging indoors. The flowering period is late summer and autumn when many other annuals are going over.

There are several good varieties including 'Goldilocks', with double and semi-double blooms in rich golden-orange, on long stems; 'Marmalade', rich golden-orange flowers with black centres; and 'Rustic Dwarfs' in gold, bronze and mahogany shades.

CULTIVATION
Easily grown in any well-drained soil and full sun. May need a few short twiggy sticks for support. Stands up well to adverse weather conditions. Watch out for slugs and snails.

PROPAGATION
Sow seeds under glass or indoors in early to mid-spring, transplant seedlings to trays, harden before planting out in late spring.

Tagetes erecta
African Marigold

Spread 30–45cm (12–18in)
Height 30–90cm (12–36in)   **HHA**

African Marigolds are extremely popular for summer
bedding. They make an incredible show, flowering
continuously from early summer until the frosts start in
autumn.

They are often mass planted in beds, especially the dwarf
ones; the dwarfs can also be grown in tubs and window
boxes; and they can be planted in bold groups in an annual
border, particularly the tall varieties. The flowers last well
when cut and arranged indoors.

There are dozens of varieties to choose from, such as the
'Inca' series. These are dwarfs, attaining about 35cm (14in)
in height, and include 'Inca Orange' which has enormous
ball-like double flowers of bright orange; 'Inca Yellow', the
bright yellow counterpart of 'Inca Orange'; and 'Inca Gold'
in a rich golden-yellow. It is also possible to buy a mixture of
'Inca' varieties.

The 'Galore' series is popular in the USA and also available
in Britain. They have huge double flowers and grow to about
45cm (18in) in height. There's 'Gold Galore' in
golden-yellow and 'Yellow Galore', a good clear yellow.

The Jubilee series is highly recommended, with large
double flowers and growing to about 60cm (24in). They are
known in America as 'hedge marigolds' and are vigorous
bushy plants with good wind resistance. Varieties are
'Diamond Jubilee', bright yellow; 'Golden Jubilee', golden
yellow; and 'Jubilee Mixed', which includes yellow,
golden-yellow and orange.

The 'Perfection' series has double flowers and reaches
35cm (14in) in height. 'Perfection Gold' is compact,
vigorous, free-flowering and highly resistant to bad weather.

The large rounded flowers are packed with golden-yellow
petals.

The 'Climax' series is tall, up to 76cm (30in), with large
fully double flowers. Colours include yellow, gold, pale
yellow and orange.

'Toreador' grows to 76cm (30in) and carries huge double
rich orange flowers.

CULTIVATION
Marigolds grow best in a
reasonably fertile soil but will
also succeed in poor dry
conditions. Full sun is needed.
Regularly cut off dead flower
heads to encourage more
blooms to follow. Guard against
slugs and snails.

PROPAGATION
Sow seeds under glass or
indoors during early or
mid-spring. Transplant
seedlings to trays or small pots;
harden and plant out when the
danger of frost is over.

Tagetes patula
French Marigold

Spread 20–30cm (8–12in)
Height 15–30cm (6–12in)

HHA

The French Marigolds are as popular as the Africans. They are also used for summer bedding, being mass planted in beds where they make a continuous show from early summer until the frosts of autumn put a stop to the display.

They can also be used for edging beds and are ideally suited to containers such as tubs and window boxes. French Marigolds can also be planted in hanging baskets.

All varieties are dwarf and may have fully double or single flowers. The main colour is yellow but other colours are available.

'Honeycomb' grows to 25cm (10in) high and has fully double crested blooms in yellow and reddish orange – a variegated effect. The flowers really glow.

The 'Queen' series is highly recommended. These are camellia-flowered marigolds and attain a height of around 30cm (12in). 'Queen Sophia' is dark apricot-orange and red while 'Scarlet Sophia' has vermilion-red blooms. Also available is a 'Queen Mixture'.

'Yellow Jacket' is a crested marigold with large double blooms in mid-yellow and it grows to a height of 20cm (8in). 'Susie Wong' has large single flowers in deep yellow and attains about 30cm (12in) in height.

'Cinnabar' grows to 30cm (12in), has superb large single blooms in scarlet and comes into bloom early. 'Seven Star Red' is a triploid hybrid – that is, it is unable to produce seeds so it puts all its energy into flowering. It grows to 30cm (12in) in height and has beautifully ruffled, fully double, mahogany red blooms at least 7.5cm (3in) across. It is extremely early and most impressive when mass planted.

The 'Boy' series is also recommended, with double flowers, such as 'Orange Boy', 15cm (6in), deep orange, and 'Boy-O-Boy Mixed', 15cm (6in), in golden-yellow, pure yellow and mahogany/gold.

There are many others that could be recommended so have a look through the catalogues to see what takes your fancy. Look out, too, for the 'Bonanza' series.

CULTIVATION
Provide a reasonably fertile soil, although plants will succeed in poor dry conditions. Full sun is needed. Regularly cut off dead flower heads to encourage more blooms to follow. Guard against slugs and snails.

PROPAGATION
Sow seeds under glass or indoors during early or mid-spring. Transplant seedlings to trays; harden and plant out when the danger of frost is over.

Tagetes tenuifolia (T. signata)
Tagetes

Spread 20–30cm (8–12in)
Height 20–30cm (8–12in)

HHA

This is a neat bushy annual with light green feathery foliage and a long succession of small flowers, produced in such profusion that they almost obscure the foliage. It's a popular plant for summer bedding, particularly for edging beds, and for colour in tubs, window boxes and hanging baskets.

Flower colours include orange, yellow, golden-yellow and red. One can buy varieties in single colours or in mixtures. The orange, yellow or golden-yellow varieties make a particularly attractive edging for a bed or blue or purple petunias or heliotrope. They are often used, too, with the wax begonia, whose flowers are red, pink or white.

Tagetes can also be recommended for the mixed border as they are useful for filling gaps at the front. In this instance they can be planted in bold informal groups, ideally associating them with blue-flowered shrubs or perennials, or with purple-leaved shrubs. They would not look too much out of place on the larger rock garden, where they would provide much-needed colour in summer and early autumn.

Many people prefer Tagetes to French Marigolds as the foliage is sweet smelling, whereas that of marigolds is very pungent and not to everyone's liking.

It is normally the *pumila* varieties that are grown such as 'Tangerine Gem' with large flowers of intense deep orange; 'Lemon Gem', like 'Golden Gem' in habit but with larger bright lemon-yellow flowers; 'Golden Gem', bright golden-yellow flowers on compact globular plants; 'Paprika', brilliant red petals edged with gold, tiny flowers; and 'Starfire', a mixture of reds, oranges and yellows, giving overall an incredibly brilliant effect.

CULTIVATION
Ideally grown in a fertile soil in full sun, Tagetes will also tolerate poor soils and very dry conditions. Regularly remove dead flowers, and guard against slugs.

PROPAGATION
Sow seeds under glass or indoors in early to mid-spring. Transplant seedlings to trays, eventually harden and plant out when the danger of frost is over.

Thunbergia alata
Black-eyed Susan

Spread 15cm (6in)
Height 3m (10ft)

HHA

This annual can be grown up a wall or trellis or allowed to trail from a hanging basket. The flowers are about 5cm (2in) wide and yellow with a dark brown centre. The flowering period is early summer to early autumn. Best results are obtained in a warm summer. Can also be grown in pots in a greenhouse or conservatory.

'Susie Mixed' includes several colours: orange, yellow and white self-colours and the same shades with black centres. Particularly recommended for hanging baskets.

CULTIVATION
A very well-drained soil is needed and a sheltered position in full sun. If these plants are to be grown against a wall or fence give them something to grip on to such as netting or wall trellis.

PROPAGATION
Seeds are sown under glass or indoors in early spring, ideally one per 7.5cm (3in) pot. Pot on to a 10cm (4in) pot. Harden and plant out when the danger of frost is over.

Tropaeolum peregrinum (T. canariense)
Canary Creeper

Spread 90cm (36in)
Height 3.6m (12ft)

HA

This extremely vigorous plant is really a short-lived perennial but is treated as an annual. The foliage is bluish green and in summer masses of yellow flowers are produced. Flowering generally continues well into the autumn.

Grow it up a wall or fence, providing something for it to cling to such as netting or wall trellis. Or allow it to scramble through large shrubs. It can also be grown up tall twiggy sticks in a border, particularly in a shrub or mixed border.

CULTIVATION
Needs plenty of sun and a moderately fertile soil if it is to grow to its full extent. Initially support plants with short twiggy sticks.

PROPAGATION
Sow outdoors in mid-spring where the plants are to flower. Best to sow two seeds at each position; if both germinate remove the weaker seedling.

Calendula officinalis
Pot Marigold

Spread 30cm (12in)
Height 30–60cm (12–24in)

HA

The Pot Marigold is an old-fashioned hardy annual which was a familiar sight in cottage gardens of the past. It is still as popular as ever but in recent years many new and improved varieties have appeared, most being of dwarf compact habit and in a wider range of colours. The traditional colour of the daisy-like flowers is orange and the flowering season is from late spring to autumn.

One of the best orange varieties is 'Orange King' with large double flowers and growing to a height of 45-60cm (18-24in).

'Fiesta Gitana' is a mixture of colours which vary from creamy yellow to deepest orange. The flowers are double, some with yellow centres others with brown. Height is 30cm (12in).

rather like chrysanthemums in a range of bright colours. Height is 60cm (24in).

A brand new mixture is 'Touch of Class', which includes peach-pink shades. The petals are bronze on the undersides. This mixture is something quite different.

Pot Marigolds have various uses: grow them in an annual or mixed border, in a cottage garden border, or even in a row in the vegetable plot specially for cutting – the blooms last well in water.

CULTIVATION
Pot Marigolds have few demands. They will grow in the poorest soils although best results are achieved in moderately fertile soils. Drainage must be good. Full sun is recommended for sturdy growth and optimum flowering. If you are growing the plants specially for cutting the terminal buds of the young plants should be cut out to encourage branching and therefore more flowers. Regularly remove dead flower heads to encourage more blooms to follow and to prevent self-seeding – marigolds can become weeds! Guard plants against slugs and snails.

PROPAGATION
Seeds are sown where the plants are to flower in early or mid-spring. Thin out the seedlings to the recommended spacing before they become overcrowded. Alternatively sow seeds in early autumn and overwinter the seedlings in the open, or under cloches in colder areas, to obtain earlier flowers the following year.

Dimorphotheca aurantiaca
Star of the Veldt

Spread 30cm (12in)
Height 30–45cm (12–18in)

HHA

Eschscholzia californica
California Poppy

Spread 15cm (6in)
Height 30cm (12in)

HA

Strictly speaking this is a perennial but it is usually grown as a half-hardy annual. It produces quite large bright orange daisy flowers in profusion from early summer to early autumn. These open only when the weather is bright and sunny – they will not open on dull days or if the plants are grown in shade.

Most seedsmen offer mixed hybrids in a range of colours including orange shades, buff, amber, gold, salmon, etc.

Use dimorphothecas for summer bedding or for the front of an annual, mixed or shrub border. They're ideal for providing summer colour on a rock garden and suitable for tubs and window boxes.

CULTIVATION
Full sun is essential, together with well-drained soil. Regularly remove dead flower heads to encourage more blooms.

PROPAGATION
Sow seeds under glass or indoors in early spring, transplant to small pots, harden off and plant out when the danger of frost is over. Alternatively sow outdoors in late spring.

This easy annual with bright poppy-like flowers will grow even in the poorest conditions. It must have plenty of sun for the flowers to open. The species itself, with bright orange flowers, is popular but mixtures such as 'Monarch Art Shades Mixed' with semi-double flowers in many brilliant colours are also widely grown. The mixture 'Ballerina' has more double and ruffled blooms.

The flowering period is from early summer to mid-autumn.

CULTIVATION
Full sun and well-drained soil are essential. Poor soils are perfectly acceptable. Pick off dead flowers before they set seeds.

PROPAGATION
Sow seeds where they are to flower, particularly in annual borders, mixed borders and on a rock garden. Sowing time is early spring, or early autumn for earlier flowers the following year.

Tithonia rotundifolia (T. speciosa)
Mexican Sunflower

Spread 30cm (12in)
Height 90cm (36in)

HHA

Ursinia pulchra (U. versicolor)
Ursinia

Spread 15cm (6in)
Height 30cm (12in)

HHA

This half-hardy annual, which is not too well-known, has attractive bright daisy flowers from mid-summer until the frosts of autumn. The colour is deep orange-red and each flower has a yellow centre. Blooms are excellent for cutting.

Good varieties are 'Goldfinger' in bright orange-scarlet and 'Torch' in the same colour.

Grow the Mexican Sunflower in an annual or mixed border, setting it fairly well back because it's a tallish plant.

CULTIVATION
The Mexican Sunflower flourishes in any soil with good drainage provided the site is in full sun. Regularly cut off dead flower heads and provide twiggy sticks for support.

PROPAGATION
Sow seeds in late winter or early spring under glass or indoors. Transplant to trays and plant out when the danger of frost is over, after hardening.

This is a charming bushy annual with feathery deep green leaves and brilliant orange flowers, each with a purplish zone. The flowering period is from early to late summer.

Ideal for the annual or mixed border and even for the larger rock garden.

CULTIVATION
Ursinia prefers a light sandy soil and it must be given a position in full sun. Picking off the dead flower heads will encourage more blooms to follow.

PROPAGATION
Seeds are sown in early spring under glass or indoors and should be only lightly covered with compost. Transplant to trays and plant out when the danger of frost is over, after hardening.

Venidium fatuosum
Monarch of the Veldt

Spread 30cm (12in)
Height 60cm (24in)   HHA

Alonsoa warscewiczii (A. grandiflora)
Mask Flower

Spread 20cm (8in)
Height 45cm (18in)   HHA

Monarch of the Veldt has large daisy flowers in deep orange, each with a brown central zone. The flowering period is early summer to mid-autumn. The foliage is also attractive, being deeply lobed and silvery in colour.

Can be mass planted in summer bedding schemes or used to fill gaps in a mixed or shrub border. Suitable for growing in large tubs. The flowers are good for cutting.

CULTIVATION
Monarch of the Veldt prefers a light well-drained soil with organic matter added. A site in full sun is recommended. It is best to provide the plants with a few twiggy sticks for support and the dead flower heads should be removed.

PROPAGATION
Sow seeds under glass or indoors during early spring and transplant the seedlings to individual small pots. Harden off and plant out when the danger of frost is over. Alternatively sow outdoors in late spring and thin out resultant seedlings.

This is a bushy perennial but generally treated as a half-hardy annual. It has a long flowering season, from early summer until well into autumn, when the frosts put a stop to the display. Masses of flattish rounded red flowers are produced against a background of deep green toothed foliage.

Grow the Mask Flower in an annual border or in a mixed or shrub border. It is a fairly unusual annual but well worth growing for its profusion of flowers.

CULTIVATION
The Mask Flower likes a moisture-retentive yet well-drained soil in full sun. One can with advantage add organic matter such as peat to soils which are naturally very dry.

PROPAGATION
Sow seeds under glass or indoors during early spring. Transplant to trays and plant out when the danger of frost is over, after hardening the plants.

Amaranthus caudatus _____
Love-lies-bleeding

Spread 45cm (18in)
Height 90cm (36in)   HHA

This plant is grown for its pendulous tassels of red flowers which may be up to 45cm (18in) long. The flowering period is from mid-summer to mid-autumn.

In catalogues it is usually offered as *Amaranthus* Dark Red, with deep red blooms. Also worth growing is the variety 'Viridis' with pale green tassels, an ideal plant for a green and white planting scheme.

Love-lies-bleeding is often used in sub-tropical bedding schemes. It could also be grown in a mixed border or in large tubs.

CULTIVATION
A good deep fertile soil with manure or compost added suits this amaranthus, but reasonable results are achieved in poorer soils. Choose a position which receives plenty of sun.

PROPAGATION
Sow seeds in early spring under glass or indoors. The seedlings should be potted into individual small pots. Harden and plant out when the danger of frost is over. Alternatively sow outdoors in flowering position during mid-spring.

Amaranthus tricolor _____
Joseph's Coat

Spread 30–45cm (12–18in)
Height 60–90cm (24–36in)   HHA

This amaranthus is also recommended for sub-tropical bedding schemes and is grown for its brilliant foliage which is basically red although other colours are present. It would also make a good dot plant in summer bedding schemes to give height and contrast. Also suitable for growing in large tubs.

It makes a bushy plant and the large leaves are generally oval and pointed, but can vary in shape according to variety.

It is varieties that are grown rather than the species. There are several to choose from and particularly recommended is 'Joseph's Coat', an improved form of the species with scarlet, yellow and green leaves.

'Flaming Fountains' is truly spectacular, almost overpowering, with glowing flame-coloured leaves. It is a compact base-branching plant, shorter than average at only 30cm (12in) in height. 'Molten Fire' is variegated with purple, bronze and crimson-scarlet leaves and is also a most striking variety.

CULTIVATION
A good deep fertile soil with manure or compost added suits this foliage amaranthus, but reasonable results are achieved in poorer soils. Choose a position which receives plenty of sun.

PROPAGATION
Sow seeds in early spring under glass or indoors. The seedlings should be potted into individual small pots. Harden and plant out when the danger of frost is over.

Begonia semperflorens _____
Wax Begonia

Spread 15–20cm (6–8in)
Height 15–30cm (6–12in)

HHA

Coleus blumei _____
Flame Nettle

Spread 30–45cm (12–18in)
Height 30–60cm (12–24in)

HHA

The Wax Begonia is a favourite summer bedding plant, particularly as a carpet in formal schemes, and as an edging for beds and borders. It is also good in tubs, window boxes and hanging baskets.

Flowering period from early summer until the autumn frosts, the main flower colour is red but shades of pink and white are also available, with many varieties to choose from in mixed colours.

'Cocktail' comes in a wide range of rich bright colours and the leaves are dark shining bronze. 'Orandie' mixture is similar except that the leaves are both green and bronze. Both are weather resistant, dwarf compact plants.

The 'Coco' series is highly recommended: 'Coco Ducolor' whose flowers are white edged with red, set against bronze foliage; 'Coco Pink', pink flowers and bronze foliage; 'Coco Bright Scarlet', brilliant scarlet blooms and bronze foliage; and 'Coco Mixed' with deep brown foliage and scarlet, red, white, pale and deep pink flowers.

The Flame Nettle is often thought of as a greenhouse pot plant but it is also successful as a summer bedding plant.

It is perhaps most suited to sub-tropical bedding schemes but it can also be included in normal summer bedding schemes, perhaps as a dot plant to give height and contrast. Use it also in containers such as tubs, window boxes and for the centres of hanging baskets.

Flame Nettle is a foliage plant with highly coloured leaves, the basic colour being red. It does flower but blooms should be cut off.

There are many varieties, all of which range from 30–60cm (12–24in) in height, including 'Fashion Parade' in a mixture of colours and leaf forms; 'Wizard Mixed', another brightly coloured mix with uniform rounded leaf form; 'Saber', narrow leaves in many colours; 'Dragon', a brilliant mix; and 'Carefree', a mixture of oak-leaved types. One can buy separate colours: 'Scarlet Poncho', 'Rose Wizard' and 'Red Monarch' all about 30cm high.

CULTIVATION
Wax Begonias like a fertile moisture-retentive soil so work in peat or compost before planting if your soil is light and sandy. Plants grow well in sun or partial shade.

PROPAGATION
Sow seeds under glass or indoors during late winter and do not cover them with compost because they are as fine as dust. Transplant to trays and plant out when the danger of frost is over after hardening the plants.

CULTIVATION
These plants require a well-drained yet moisture-retentive soil and full sun or partial shade. Guard against slugs and snails.

PROPAGATION
Sow seeds in early spring under glass or indoors, transplant to trays and harden thoroughly before planting out when the frosts have finished.

Cosmos bipinnatus _____
Cosmos

Spread 60cm (24in)
Height 30–90cm (12–36in)　　　**HHA**

A popular annual for borders and for cutting. It has finely cut foliage and large rounded flowers in shades of red and pink. Flowering period is mid- to late summer to early autumn.

　Recommended varieties are 'Candytripe', 75cm (30in), white flowers striped red; and 'Sensation', 90cm (36in), a mix of red, pink and white. Also try the *C. sulphureus* varieties 'Bright Lights', 75cm (30in), a mix of gold, orange and scarlet; 'Diablo', 60cm (24in), orange-red; 'Sunny Gold', 40cm (16in), golden-yellow; and 'Sunny Red', 30cm (12in), orange vermilion.

CULTIVATION
Cosmos prefers a light well-drained poor soil and full sun and does not do so well in wet summers. Tall varieties will need supports, and remove the dead flower heads.

PROPAGATION
Sow seeds under glass or indoors in late winter/early spring; transplant seedlings to trays; harden well and plant out after frosts.

Glaucium corniculatum _____
Horned Poppy

Spread 30cm (12in)
Height 25cm (10in)　　　**HA**

This is not one of the best-known annuals but it is well worth growing in a mixed or shrub border. It produces crimson poppy flowers in summer and has deeply cut downy foliage.

CULTIVATION
Any ordinary garden soil is suitable provided the drainage is good. An open position in full sun is needed.

PROPAGATION
Sow seeds in early to mid-spring where the plants are to flower. Thin out the seedlings before they become overcrowded. Do not attempt to transplant seedlings as they do not always re-establish – they dislike root disturbance. Seeds should have only a light covering of soil.

53

Impatiens wallerana (I. holstii)
Busy Lizzie

Spread 30cm (12in)
Height 15–30cm (6–12in)

HHA

The Busy Lizzie has become very popular as a summer
bedding plant. Formerly it was mainly grown as a
greenhouse pot plant.

Many new varieties have been produced in recent years,
these being of dwarf compact habit and in a wide range of
colours. The basic colour is red and impatiens comes in all
shades of this. Pink shades are prominent and there are also
orange shades and white.

Flowering is continuous from early summer until the
autumn frosts put a stop to the display. The plants smother
themselves with blooms, hiding most of the foliage.

Busy Lizzies can be mass planted in summer bedding
schemes (particularly in sub-tropical schemes), grown in
ornamental containers such as tubs, window boxes and
hanging baskets and do not look out of place planted in bold
drifts among shrubs or perennials.

There are many varieties worth growing including the
'Super Elfin' series, which includes 'Lipstick', 20cm (8in)
high with large rose-red flowers. It's very early, compact and
free flowering. Other varieties in this series are 'Blush',
'Orange', 'Red', 'Salmon', 'Fuchsia', 'Orchid Blue' and
'White'.

'Blitz', 15cm (6in), has extra-large orange-scarlet flowers
and bronze-green foliage.

'Novette Mixed' is popular, at 10cm (4in) high. The mix
includes many bright colours and the flowers are large.
Separate colours are also available.

The 'Rosette Hybrids', 15cm (6in), have double and semi
double flowers and colours include scarlet, rose, salmon,
pink and white. 'Confection Mixed', 20cm (8in), has mainly
double flowers and colours include red, orange, pink and

rose. This is a considerable improvement on the 'Rosette
Hybrids'.

'Accent' is another highly recommended mix and has
large flowers appearing early in the season.

CULTIVATION
A moisture-retentive soil is best
so add plenty of bulky organic
matter if you have a light soil
which rapidly dries out. Grow in
full sun, partial shade or full
shade. Keep well supplied with
water in summer.

PROPAGATION
Sow seeds in early spring under
glass or indoors. Do not cover
seeds with compost because
they are as fine as dust.
Transplant to trays; harden and
plant out after frosts.

Linum grandiflorum
Annual Flax

Spread 15cm (6in)
Height 30–45cm (12–18in)

HA

The Annual Flax or *Linum grandiflorum* is a popular and most attractive hardy annual with several uses. It is, of course, a suitable candidate for the annual border. However, it would not look out of place in the mixed border as it associates well with hardy herbaceous perennials and with shrubs.

Try the Annual Flax, too, on the larger rock garden where it will help to provide much-needed colour during the summer, when the majority of rock plants have finished their display. As it is a fairly tall plant, do not place it at the top of a rock garden, where it would create a rather top-heavy effect, but rather on the lower levels.

The Annual Flax is a thin-stemmed plant with light green, slender pointed leaves. These make a nice foil for the small bowl-shaped rose-red flowers which are freely produced between early and late summer.

Although the species is sometimes available, the variety 'Rubrum' is usually grown and it is certainly more showy than the species. It is popularly known as the Scarlet Flax due to its brilliant scarlet flowers.

CULTIVATION

Flax is easily grown and will thrive in any ordinary garden soil provided the drainage is good. If drainage needs improving then work into the soil a liberal dressing of coarse horticultural sand or grit. This will open up the soil and allow surplus water to easily drain to lower levels.

Flax enjoys lime in the soil although this is not essential for its well-being.

Full sun, though, is necessary for optimum flowering so choose an open position which receives sun for best part of the day.

As the stems of Flax are rather thin, a few short twiggy sticks may be needed for support, particularly if the garden is prone to winds. Thin-stemmed plants are particularly prone to being flattened by wind when they are heavy with rain.

PROPAGATION

Seeds should be sown where the plants are to flower, the best time being early spring. Before the seedlings start to become overcrowded they should be thinned out.

Alternatively make a sowing in early autumn if you have a very well-drained soil and live in a comparitively mild area. The plants are overwintered out of doors, ideally with a covering of cloches, and will produce earlier blooms the following year.

Pelargonium x hortorum
Zonal Geranium

Spread 30–45cm (12–18in)
Height 30–60cm (12–24in)

HHA

The Zonal Geranium is one of the essential summer bedding plants. The modern seed-raised strains are now widely used for this purpose. Although the plants are strictly perennial they are treated as annuals and discarded in the autumn when the frosts put a stop to the display. Flowering is continuous throughout summer.

The Zonal Geranium is mass planted in formal summer bedding schemes, in tubs and window boxes and can be used as a centrepiece for hanging baskets.

The main colour is red, which comes in all shades. The flowers are brilliant and need toning down with suitable dot plants such as silver-leaved cineraria or the effect can be overpowering.

Other colours include shades of pink, orange and also white. There are one or two purplish varieties.

There's a great range of varieties available from seedsmen. Here we can only take a look at a few of the best.

The 'Video' series is early flowering with a compact habit of growth. It has dark foliage and comes in a bright mix of colours. Ideal for window boxes.

The 'Diamond' series is perfect for bedding and has extremely good weather resistance. The plants are compact, free flowering and early. There's 'Scarlet Diamond', bright scarlet; 'Cherry Diamond', luminous cherry red; and 'Rose Diamond', rose-red.

'Hollywood Star' is a striking white and rose bicolor and comes into flower early in the season.

The 'Orbit' series can be highly recommended and has distinct foliage zoning. It is available in mixtures or separate colours, including 'Orange Orbit', almost pure orange;

'Scarlet Orbit Improved', with large flowers; and 'White Orbit', pure white.

Last but not least, the 'Sprinter' series is slightly later and larger than the 'Diamond' series but very free flowering. 'Sprinter' itself is a glowing salmon-scarlet.

CULTIVATION
Choose a position in full sun with a moderately fertile soil. It is important regularly to pick off dead flower heads.

PROPAGATION
Sow seeds under glass or indoors as early as possible – in early or mid-winter. Transplant the seedlings to individual 7.5cm (3in) pots; pot on to 12.5cm (5in) pots; harden well and plant out when the danger of frost is over.

Ricinus communis
Castor Oil Plant

Spread 90cm (36in)
Height 1.2–1.5m (4–5ft)

HHA

Salvia splendens
Scarlet Sage

Spread 20–30cm (8–12in)
Height 30cm (12in)

HHA

The Castor Oil Plant is excellent for giving height to formal summer bedding schemes. There's no better foliage plant for sub-tropical schemes and it does not look out of place in a shrub or mixed border.

It has large palmate leaves, green in the species but bronzy in the several varieties. The variety 'Gibsonii' has beautiful bronze foliage and is more compact in habit than the species. 'Impala' is a newer variety, again with striking bronze leaves.
Warning: all parts of the plant (including seeds) are poisonous.

CULTIVATION
A reasonably fertile soil well enriched with organic matter such as garden compost or peat is best. Full sun is ideal but it does quite well in partial shade. Provide bamboo canes for support particularly if the garden is prone to winds.

PROPAGATION
Sow seeds in late winter or early spring, under glass or indoors. It is best to sow one seed per 7.5cm (3in) pot and later to pot on to 12.5cm (5in) pots. Harden well before planting out when the danger of frost is over.

This is one of the most popular summer bedding plants with its brilliant scarlet blooms throughout summer.

There are many to choose from and some of the best include 'Blaze of Fire', vivid scarlet, early and compact, a most popular variety; 'Carabiniere', deep crimson blooms and dark green foliage; 'Red Riches' ('Ryco'). dazzling scarlet spikes on compact plants, dark green foliage, early flowering; 'Red Hot Sally', small plants, early flowering, brilliant scarlet, highly popular in N. America; 'Caramba', scarlet; and 'Dress Parade Mixed', an eye-catching mix of scarlet, rose, pink, purple and white, early flowering and of dwarf habit. A bright deep purple variety is 'Laser Purple' which makes a good contrast with the scarlet varieties.

CULTIVATION
Any reasonable, well-drained garden soil is suitable for salvias. A position which receives plenty of sun is recommended for optimum growth and flowering. The tips of young plants should be pinched out when they are about 7.5cm (3in) high to encourage side shoots and hence more flowers. Regularly cut off dead flowers to encourage more to follow. This is a bit tedious but well worth doing.

PROPAGATION
Sow seeds in late winter or early spring in a greenhouse or indoors. The seedlings should be transplanted to trays before they become overcrowded. Grow on the young plants in warm conditions – no lower than 10°C (50°F) and harden thoroughly before planting out when the danger of frost is over.

Agrostemma githago
Corn Cockle

Spread 20cm (8in)
Height 60–90cm (24–36in)

HA

Clarkia elegans
Clarkia

Spread 30cm (12in)
Height 30–60cm (12–24in)

HA

The wild Corn Cockle is a weed in southern Europe and is not grown in gardens. There is, however, an attractive variety of the wild species which is a popular hardy annual. It is called 'Milas' and bears rose-pink flowers during the summer. These make a good show if the plants are grown in a group. It should be noted that the seeds of the Corn Cockle are poisonous.

Grow the Corn Cockle in an annual border, or sow in bold groups in a mixed border or shrubbery.

CULTIVATION
Full sun is needed for optimum growth and flowering. Any ordinary garden soil is suitable provided the drainage is good. The Corn Cockle actually prefers a limy or chalky soil but this is not essential. Provide twiggy sticks for support.

PROPAGATION
Seeds are sown where the plants are to flower during early spring. Thin out the seedlings before they become overcrowded. Alternatively make a sowing in early autumn and overwinter the seedlings under cloches in cold areas. You will then get earlier flowers.

This is one of the most popular of the hardy annuals and is easily grown. It makes a good show from mid-summer to early autumn and can be grown in an annual or mixed border. It's excellent for cutting and for this purpose could even be grown in a row in the vegetable garden.

The double flowers are produced in spikes and the predominant colour is pink. It is generally sold as a mixture including shades of pink, red, salmon, lavender, purple, orange and white.

Also worth growing is *Clarkia pulchella*, again sold as a mix of several colours which include rose-pink, violet and white.

CULTIVATION
Clarkia thrives in a light well-drained soil, on the acid side preferably although this is not essential. Full sun is needed, and do not be too generous with the fertilizer because this can result in fewer flowers.

PROPAGATION
Sow seeds in early spring in the open where the plants are to flower. Thin out seedlings before overcrowding occurs. Alternatively sow outdoors in early autumn and overwinter under cloches in cold areas.

Cleome spinosa
Spider Flower

Spread 45cm (18in)
Height 1.2m (4ft)   HHA

Dianthus chinensis
Annual Pinks

Spread 15cm (6in)
Height 15–20cm (6–8in)   HHA

This is quite a bushy plant with spiny stems and pink and white spidery flowers from mid-summer until the frosts of autumn put a stop to the display. There is a variety named 'Rose Queen' with rose-pink flowers. 'Colour Fountains' is a mix of colours: pink, rose-pink, lilac, purple and white.

The Spider Flower can be used in formal bedding schemes as a dot plant to give height and contrast and it's an excellent subject for a mixed or shrub border.

CULTIVATION
It needs a rich well-drained soil containing plenty of humus, provided by adding garden compost or peat. It's absolutely essential to choose a position in full sun.

PROPAGATION
Seeds should be sown under glass or indoors during early spring. Transplant seedlings to individual 9cm (3½in) pots. Thoroughly harden before planting out in late spring.

Pinks are favourite plants for mixed borders, for cottage gardens and for bedding out. They bloom from mid-summer until the autumn.

Recommended varieties of pinks are: 'Magic Charms', which provides sturdy plants covered with large single flowers in bright and showy colours; 'Telstar', which is very early and free flowering in a mixture of many brilliant colours; and 'Lace Mixed' with its distinctive fringed lacy flowers in several shades, including white.

The annual carnations, varieties of *Dianthus caryophyllus*, can be included here, and we recommend the 'Knight' series, extra compact, with large fully double flowers on strong stems. 'Scarlet Luminette' has well-shaped double flowers in bright scarlet and is specially good for cutting. And 'Chabaud's Giant Mixed' grows to 45cm (18in) in height and has fully double large flowers in various shades of pink and red. This is excellent for cutting.

CULTIVATION
Provide well-drained soil, and, although any type is suitable, alkaline soils are particularly relished by pinks and carnations. Full sun is needed for optimum growth and flowering.

PROPAGATION
Sow seeds in late winter or early spring under glass or indoors. When seedlings are large enough to handle pot them individually into 7.5cm (3in) pots.

Digitalis purpurea _____
Common Foxglove

Spread 45–60cm (18–24in)
Height 1.5m (5ft)

HB

Godetia grandiflora _____
Godetia

Spread 15cm (6in)
Height 30cm (12in)

HA

The Foxglove is a native of Britain and in early to mid-summer produces tall spikes of pink tubular flowers. It is a woodland plant and an ideal place to grow it in the garden is in a shrub border. Strictly speaking it is a short-lived perennial. Try the 'Excelsior' strain with pink, purple, cream and white flowers, all handsomely spotted with brown.

CULTIVATION
Foxgloves will grow in any type of soil and grow best in moisture-retentive soils so add plenty of bulky organic matter if you have a light soil.

Partial shade, particularly dappled shade as cast by trees, is better than a position in full sun. Full or deep shade, however, can lead to weak growth.

PROPAGATION
Although seeds can be sown in the open it is more convenient to germinate them under glass in seed trays, for they are tiny. Make the sowing in late spring and germinate in a cool greenhouse or cold frame. It's best not to cover the seeds with compost because this can prevent germination. When the seedlings are large enough to handle easily, transplant them either to other seed trays or direct into a nursery bed in the open ground. If you have transplanted into trays, the plants still need to go eventually into the nursery bed before the young plants become overcrowded.

Set out the plants in their flowering positions in early to mid-autumn.

These are popular bushy annuals whose bright flowers, mainly in shades of pink and which are produced from early to late summer, are excellent for cutting. They are best grown in an annual or mixed border.

Several varieties are available, some with single flowers, others double. Particularly recommended are 'Double Mixed', 'Azalea-Flowered Mixed' whose semi-double blooms are rather like those of azaleas; and 'Monarch' ('Dwarf Gem') mixture.

CULTIVATION
For best results choose a position in full sun. A light sandy soil is preferred but whatever the type it must be well drained. Ensure that the soil is not too rich or the plants will produce fewer flower and a lot of foliage.

PROPAGATION
Sow the seeds in early or mid-spring where the plants are to flower. Thin out before overcrowding occurs. Alternatively for early blooms next year make a sowing outdoors in early autumn. In cold areas the seedlings should be covered with cloches during the winter.

Helipterum roseum (Acroclinium roseum) _____
Australian Everlasting

Spread 15cm (6in)
Height 45cm (18in)   HA

Iberis umbellata _____
Candytuft

Spread 20cm (8in)
Height 15–30cm (6–12in)   HA

The Australian Everlasting has strawy, daisy-like flowers in rose-pink between early and late summer. Most people grow this purely for cutting, in which case it could be given a row in the vegetable plot, but it also makes a good show in an annual or mixed border.

CULTIVATION
Good results are obtained on poor dry soils and a position in full sun. In any event the plant should not be given too rich a soil so do not worry about applying fertilizer before sowing.

The flowers are particularly suitable for drying and using in winter arrangements, and they should be cut before they have fully opened. Bundle the flowers loosely and hang them upside down for a few weeks in a cool dry airy place to thoroughly dry them.

PROPAGATION
Sow the seeds in mid-spring where the plants are to flower. Before the seedlings become overcrowded thin them out to the correct distance apart.

This is a popular hardy annual which is easily grown. The clusters of flowers come mainly in shades of pink but there are other colours too, such as shades or red, purple and also white. Generally Candytuft is offered in mixes of colours.

The following varieties are recommended: 'Fairy Maid', height 20cm (8in), with flowers in various colours; and 'White Pinnacle' which is popular for cut flowers.

Candytuft is an excellent choice for the front of an annual border, and for filling gaps in the front of mixed borders. Some people grow Candytuft in rock gardens where it will provide much-needed colour from early summer to early autumn.

Candytuft is also a good choice for ornamental containers such as tubs and window boxes and is often grown with other small hardy annuals.

CULTIVATION
Candytuft grows in virtually any kind of soil but as with all annuals the drainage must be good. If you have a poor-quality soil do not worry – Candytuft will still thrive. A position in full sun will ensure plenty of flowers.

PROPAGATION
Sow seeds where they are to flower in early spring and thin out the seedlings before they become overcrowded. To maintain a succession of flowers make further sowings in mid- and late spring. To provide early flowers make a sowing in early autumn and overwinter the young plants under cloches if you live in a cold area.

Lavatera trimestris (L. rosea) _____
Annual Mallow

Spread 45cm (18in)
Height 60–90cm (24–36in)   HA

Malcolmia maritima _____
Virginian Stock

Spread 15cm (6in)
Height 15cm (6in)   HA ☀ ✳ S

This is an easy and showy hardy annual suitable for growing in the annual or mixed border.

There are several excellent varieties including 'Silver Cup' which grows to 90cm (36in) in height. Like all Annual Mallows it flowers from mid-summer to early autumn. By mid-summer the substantial bushy plants are a mass of glowing deep rose-pink flowers, each bloom beautifully veined with a deeper shade. It's one of the best for cut flowers, and it's little wonder that this superb variety has gained an award in European flower trials. Another excellent variety that has also fared well in European trials is 'Mont Blanc'; This grows to about 60cm (24in) in height and is a glistening pure white companion to 'Silver Cup'.

CULTIVATION
Any ordinary garden soil is suitable for the Annual Mallows provided it is well drained. Too rich a soil can lead to excess foliage at the expense of flowers. So do not add fertilizer before sowing or farmyard manure, or garden compost.

A position in full sun is essential for optimum flowering and the site should be sheltered from winds.

PROPAGATION
Sow the seeds in mid-spring where the plants are to flower, and cover very lightly with fine soil. As soon as the seedlings are large enough to handle thin them out. Alternatively, for early flowers the following year make a sowing in early autumn.

This is one of the easiest and best-known of all the hardy annuals. It's an ideal subject for the front of borders (annual or mixed) where it is best sown in bold groups or drifts for maximum impact.

Available in a mixture of colours, mainly shades of pink but including lilac, red and white shades and creamy yellow. The flowers are small, only about 12mm ($\frac{1}{2}$in) in diameter and are carried on thin stems in summer. The flowers start to appear about one month after sowing and the flowering period lasts for approximately two months. This is an ideal annual for impatient children to grow because it matures so quickly.

CULTIVATION
Any ordinary garden soil is suitable for the Virginian Stock provided it drains well. A sunny site is best although good results are possible in partial shade. The plants self-sow themselves quite freely.

PROPAGATION
The seeds are sown where the plants are to flower. Make a sowing in early spring and further sowings up to mid-summer to ensure a succession of flowers. Another sowing could be made in early autumn to provide early flowers the following year. Only lightly cover the seeds with fine soil.

Silene pendula
Nodding Catchfly

Spread 15cm (6in)
Height 15–20cm (6–8in)　　**HA**

Brachycome iberidifolium
Swan River Daisy

Spread 30cm (12in)
Height 30–45cm (12–18in)　　**HHA**  **S**

A useful hardy annual for borders, particularly for filling gaps at the front of mixed borders. It is a neat compact grower with small star-shaped flowers in pale pink produced between late spring and early autumn, the exact period depending on when the seeds are sown.

This is also a suitable annual for sowing on rock gardens to fill any gaps and it looks good, too, growing in gaps in paving, particularly in a cottage garden

CULTIVATION
The Nodding Catchfly will grow in any ordinary garden soil provided it drains well. Best results are achieved in a sunny position but plants also do reasonably well in partial shade.

PROPAGATION
Seeds are sown where they are to flower in early or mid-spring. Thin out the seedlings before they become overcrowded. Also make another sowing in early autumn if you want early blooms the following year, but in cold areas overwinter under cloches.

This is a charming little plant for the front of annual or mixed borders. It also makes a good cut flower and has daisy-shaped blooms. Often the variety 'Purple Splendour' is grown which has purple-blue flowers. There is also a mixture with flowers in purple, blue, mauve and white.

Try growing the Swan River Daisy on the rock garden. The flowering period is early summer to early autumn.

CULTIVATION
Provide a sheltered spot in full sun. A fairly fertile soil gives the best results although the plants will grow in any ordinary well-drained garden soil. The growing tips of young plants should be cut out to encourage a bushy habit. Short twiggy sticks will be needed to support the plants, which have thin stems.

PROPAGATION
Seeds are sown under glass or indoors during early spring, being covered only lightly with fine compost. Transplant to trays and after hardening plant out when the danger of frost is over. Alternatively sow outdoors in mid-spring where the plants are to flower and thin out the seedlings before they become overcrowded.

Cobaea scandens _____
Cup and Saucer Vine

Spread 60cm (24in)
Height 3m (10ft)

HHA

Although this is a tender perennial it is generally grown as an annual. It is a vigorous climber with large bell-shaped purple flowers from early summer to early autumn.

Grow the Cup and Saucer Vine up walls, fences, trellis or pergolas where it will attach itself by means of tendrils. It is also a useful climber for a large conservatory where it can be grown as a perennial.

CULTIVATION
The Cup and Saucer Vine needs a sunny sheltered position and well-drained soil. Avoid too rich a soil as this leads to vigorous lush leafy growth at the expense of flowers. Water the plant well in dry weather. If growing it on a wall or fence provide something for the tendrils to cling to such as trellis panels or netting.

PROPAGATION
Sow seeds under glass or indoors in early or mid-spring, one seed per 7.5cm (3in) pot. Use soil-based potting compost. Pot on to a 12.5cm (5in) pot; harden thoroughly and plant out in early summer when all danger of frost is over.

Lunaria annua (L. biennis) _____
Honesty

Spread 30cm (12in)
Height 75–90cm (30–36in)

HB **S**

Honesty is a popular biennial and a typical cottage-garden plant. It also looks good in a mixed or shrub border. The purple flowers are scented, produced in the period mid-spring to early summer and are followed by round flat silvery seed pods which are often cut and dried for use in winter flower arrangements. There is a variety called 'Munstead Purple' which has large rosy purple blooms.

CULTIVATION
Partial shade is recommended. The seed heads, if required for drying, should be cut in late summer before they become damaged by inclement weather.

PROPAGATION
Sow the seeds outdoors in a spare piece of ground during late spring or early summer. The seedlings then should be transplanted to another plot before they become overcrowded, spacing them 15cm (6in) apart in a row. The young plants are finally set out in their flowering positions in early autumn.

Malope trifida 'Grandiflora' _____
Mallow-wort

Spread 25cm (10in)
Height 90cm (36in)

HA

This hardy annual is of upright bushy habit and produces rose-purple trumpet-shaped blooms during early summer to early autumn. The blooms are excellent for cutting and last well in water if gathered just as they open.

This a colourful plant for borders, whether annual or mixed.

CULTIVATION
The Mallow-wort should be grown in a position in full sun. Any ordinary garden soil is suitable but a light soil is preferred, and certainly should have good drainage. If necessary, provide twiggy sticks for support.

PROPAGATION
Early or mid-spring is the sowing period. And the seeds should be sown outdoors where the plants are to flower. Cover the seeds only lightly with fine soil. Before overcrowding occurs thin out the seedlings to the recommended spacing.

Nierembergia caerulea (N. hippomanica) _____
Cup Flower

Spread 15–20cm (6–8in)
Height 15–20cm (6-8in)

HHA

Strictly speaking this is a tender perennial but it is normally grown as a half-hardy annual. It is a charming little plant with a profusion of funnel-shaped mauve flowers from early summer to early autumn. Usually the variety 'Purple Robe' is grown, which has brilliant purplish-violet blooms.

Grow it as an edging in a mixed or annual border or in a summer bedding scheme. It is also good for filling any gaps on rock gardens.

CULTIVATION
Choose a spot in full sun and sheltered from wind because these plants are easily damaged. Any ordinary garden soil is suitable, and the plant likes moisture.

PROPAGATION
Sow under glass in late winter or early spring and transplant the seedlings to trays. Before planting outdoors, when the danger of frost is over, thoroughly harden the plants. This plant can also be propagated from soft, 5cm (2in) long cuttings taken in summer and rooted in pots of cutting compost in a cold frame. Pot on when well rooted into 7.5cm (3in) pots of soil-based potting compost and overwinter in a cold frame or indoors. Pinch out growing tips of young plants to encourage bushy growth.

Ageratum houstonianum
Floss Flower

Spread 15–30cm (6–12in)
Height 15–30cm (6–12in)

HHA

The Floss Flower is as popular as Zonal Geraniums, Scarlet Salvias and Wax Begonias and is often grown with these plants.

It is an admirable plant for the main carpet in a planned bed, mixed with other dwarf plants such as Wax Begonias and Salvias. Alternatively it can be used to edge a bed and looks best if planted in a wide band, at least 10cm (12in) across, rather than in a thin strip.

The Floss Flower combines well with other summer bedding plants in tubs, window boxes and hanging baskets. A bold drift in a shrub border is also most effective. The taller varieties are suitable for cutting because the blooms last well in water, and they are often used in miniature or small arrangements.

Ageratum is a dwarf compact plant with mounds of fluffy flowers from early summer until the frosts put a stop to the display. Once started, the plants are never out of flower. Blue is the main colour but there are other colours such as mauve, purple, pink and white.

Good varieties include 'Blue Mink', 25cm (9in) high, with large trusses of powder-blue flowers on upright compact plants; 'Ocean', 20cm (8in) high, light blue, early and extremely free flowering; 'Summer Snow', 15cm (6in), pure white flowers covering uniform plants; 'Blue Danube', 15–20cm (6–8in) high, early lavender-blue flowers on uniform plants; and 'North Sea', 20cm (8in) high, deep violet-blue flowers freely produced.

CULTIVATION

The Floss Flower should be grown in full sun and appreciates some shelter from the wind. The soil should be capable of retaining moisture during drought periods because dry conditions can lead to poor growth and flowering, and a shorter flowering period. Therefore, when preparing or digging beds, add plenty of bulky organic matter such as garden compost, peat or pulverized bark, especially if your soil is on the light side and prone to drying out. Apply a general-purpose or flower-garden fertilizer before planting to ensure fertile conditions, which result in better growth.

To encourage continuous flowering it is advisable to cut off dead flower heads regularly, using a pair of gardening scissors. Do not try to pull them off or you will uproot the plants.

Keep the plants well watered in dry periods if the soil starts to dry out.

PROPAGATION

Sow seeds under glass or indoors during early or mid-spring. Transplant to trays and plant out when the danger of frost is over, and the plants have been well hardened.

Anchusa capensis
Summer Forget-me-not

Spread 15–20cm (6–8in)
Height 25–45cm (10–18in)

HA HB

Centaurea cyanus
Cornflower

Spread 20–30cm (8–12in)
Height 45–90cm (18–36in)

HA

This is a biennial which is normally grown as a hardy annual. It has a bushy habit up to 45cm (18in) in height and bears blue flowers from mid-summer to late summer. There is a good variety named 'Blue Angel' which grows to only 25cm (10in) in height, whose flowers are also in a beautiful shade of blue.

The species makes a fine show in an annual or mixed border while the dwarf variety can be used as an edging and, combined with other plants, it does well in tubs and window boxes.

CULTIVATION
Any ordinary garden soil suits anchusa provided the drainage is good; and it needs a position in full sun.

PROPAGATION
Sow seeds where the plants are to flower during mid-spring, then thin out the resultant seedlings to the recommended spacing. If you grow the plant as a biennial sow outdoors in late summer, thin out the seedlings, and overwinter the young plants under cloches.

The Cornflower is a real favourite; it is easily grown, it makes a fine show from early summer to early autumn and its flowers are good for cutting. Often grown in an annual border it is also effective in a mixed border of perennials and shrubs.

The daisy-like double flowers are commonly blue but other colours are available including shades of red, pink purple and white.

Good varieties include 'Blue Diadem', 60cm (24in) high, with large double flowers of the richest blue; 'Jubilee Gem', 45cm (18in) high, with deep blue double flowers on bushy plants, ideal for mass planting in bold groups; and 'Polka Dot Mixed', 38cm (15in) high, with double flowers in shades of blue, red, pink and white.

CULTIVATION
Cornflowers require a fertile soil to reach their maximum potential. So, add well-rotted farmyard manure or garden compost to the soil while preparing it and rake in a dressing of general purpose or flower-garden fertilizer before sowing. A position in full sun is essential for optimum flowering.

Provide the plants with twiggy sticks for support, particularly the taller varieties, or they may be flattened by wind and rain.

PROPAGATION
Sow seeds during early or mid-spring where the plants are to flower and thin out the seedlings to the recommended spacing before they start to become overcrowded.

Alternatively, make a sowing in early autumn to provide earlier flowers in the following year. In cold areas the plants should be overwintered under cloches.

Convolvulus tricolor (C. minor)
Dwarf Morning Glory

Spread 15–20cm (6–8in)
Height 30cm (12in)

HA

A low bushy annual with large wide trumpet-shaped flowers from mid-summer to early autumn, which are a brilliant blue with a white centre. Although each flower does not last for more than a day, plenty more follow, so flowering is continuous.

Good varieties include 'Blue Flash', 20cm (8in) high, a beautiful shade of blue with white centres; and 'Royal Ensign', 30cm (12in) high, deep bright ultramarine blue, extremely free flowering. There are also mixtures of colours available which include shades of pink, red and blue.

Ideal for mass planting in beds, it is also suitable for use as edging or for filling gaps on a rock garden.

It is also a good annual for ornamental containers where it will partially spill over the edges. If you have a steep sunny bank try mass planting the Dwarf Morning Glory on it where it will make a stunning display. The warmth, coupled with well-drained conditions, will be very much to its liking and it should romp away, producing a beautiful blue 'waterful'.

In ideal conditions the Dwarf Morning Glory can self-sow itself, so if your garden is in a mild or hot climate you may well never be without plants once you have made the first sowing.

The Dwarf Morning Glory also makes an excellent pot plant for the conservatory provided it receives enough sun. It will enjoy the extra warmth and will flower throughout summer and well into the autumn.

CULTIVATION
Provided the drainage is good any ordinary garden soil is suitable for the Dwarf Morning Glory. Full sun, however, is needed for optimum flowering.

To encourage more blooms pick off the dead flower heads regularly.

PROPAGATION
Seeds can be sown under glass or indoors during early spring and young plants set out in late spring after thorough hardening; alternatively, make a sowing in mid-spring where the plants are to flower; it can also be sown in early autumn and overwintered under cloches.

Didiscus caerulea
Blue Lace Flower

Spread 20cm (8in)
Height 45cm (18in)

 HHA

Felicia bergerana
Kingfisher Daisy

Spread 15cm (6in)
Height 15cm (6in)

 HHA

This is an upright annual, useful both for annual or mixed borders and for growing specially for cutting. It has deeply cut foliage and between mid- and late summer produces rounded heads of lavender blue flowers, similar to those of scabious.

CULTIVATION
The Blue Lace Flower is an undemanding plant, but prefers a position in full sun and a well-drained soil that is reasonably fertile. Try to provide a sheltered spot and support the stems with twiggy sticks.

PROPAGATION
Seeds should be sown in early spring under glass or indoors and covered only lightly with fine compost. Transplant to 7.5cm (3in) pots (or trays if preferred), harden thoroughly and plant out when the danger of frost is over.

This is a charming little annual with blue daisy flowers from early summer to early autumn. It looks good mass planted as the main carpet in a formal design, and makes a change from such plants as Ageratum and Begonias. Use it also for edging beds and borders or plant a drift at the front of a mixed or shrub border. It is suitable, too, for the rock garden and for containers such as window boxes and urns. The blooms open fully only in the sun – they remain closed during dull weather.

CULTIVATION
Full sun is essential together with well-drained soil. Any type of soil is, however, suitable. Remove dead flower heads regularly.

PROPAGATION
Sow seeds under glass or indoors in late winter or early spring. Transplant the seedlings to individual small pots or into trays. Harden thoroughly before planting out when the danger of frost is over.

Gilia capitata
Blue Thimble Flower

Spread 20cm (8in)
Height 45cm (18in)

HA

Heliotropium arborescens (H. peruvianum)
Heliotrope

Spread 30–38cm (12–15in)
Height 45–60cm (18–24in)

HHA S

The Blue Thimble Flower has ferny green foliage and lavender-blue globular flowers from early summer to early autumn. The blooms are especially good for cutting as they last well in water. Grow it in a bold group in an annual or mixed border.

CULTIVATION
If the plants are to grow and flower well they must be given a position in full sun. Although any well-drained garden soil is suitable for gilias, they do prefer a light sandy type. It is advisable to provide twiggy sticks for support otherwise rain and winds may flatten the plants.

PROPAGATION
Sow seeds in early spring where the plants are to flower and thin out the resultant seedlings to the recommended spacing before they start to become overcrowded. Alternatively make a sowing in early autumn for early blooms the following year. It's best to protect these young plants with cloches through the winter months.

Although this is a bushy perennial it is grown as a half-hardy annual for summer bedding schemes. It has flowers in various shades of blue and one of the most popular varieties is 'Marine' which attains a height of 60cm (24in) and has extremely large heads of deep violet flowers on compact dark-leaved plants.

Heliotrope is as popular as Zonal Geraniums, Scarlet Salvias, Petunias, and Marigolds for summer bedding and is usually combined with these plants in formal schemes. It can be used as a dot plant in a carpet of plants, and also as a useful foil for those bedding plants that have strongly coloured flowers of scarlet, crimson or brilliant orange.

The flowering period of Heliotrope is late spring to mid-autumn.

CULTIVATION
Full sun is needed for best growth and flowering as is a well-drained, fertile soil. It pays to improve the soil, particularly poor light kinds, by adding bulky organic matter such as well-rotted farmyard manure, garden compost, peat or pulverized bark. Then before planting, fork into the soil a base dressing of general purpose or flower garden fertilizer. Keep well watered in dry weather and regularly pick off dead flower heads.

PROPAGATION
Sow seeds in late winter under glass. Pinch out growing tips of transplants to encourage bushy growth, and harden well before planting out after frosts are over.

Heliotrope can also be increased from cuttings taken in late summer or early autumn and rooted in heat. The young cuttings must overwinter in a frost-free greenhouse.

Ionopsidium acaule _____
Violet Cress

Spread 10cm (4in)
Height 5–7.5cm (2–3in)

HA

Ipomoea tricolor (I. rubrocoerulea) _____
Morning Glory

Spread 30cm (12in)
Height 2.4m (8ft)

HHA

This little annual is not too well known but is a good choice for sowing on the rock garden or in gaps in paving. It has a tufted habit and pale blue flowers from early summer to early autumn. The blooms are very tiny, about 6mm ($\frac{1}{4}$in) across.

CULTIVATION
Partial shade is recommended because very hot conditions can result in the little plants being scorched. Also a moist soil is necessary – one that is not prone to rapid drying out in the summer.

PROPAGATION
Sow the seeds in mid-spring and in succession, if desired, up until mid-summer. If you sow thinly you will not need to thin out the seedlings, which can be a bit tedious. Cover the seeds lightly with fine soil. If your garden is in a mild area it may be possible to overwinter young plants under cloches from an early autumn sowing. This will give you earlier flowers the following year.

This is one of the few annual climbers (or strictly speaking a tender perennial grown as an annual). The thin stems twine around supports such as pergolas or trellis and from mid-summer to early autumn bear large saucer-shaped blooms each of which lasts for only one day. But plenty more follow!

Two varieties are commonly grown; 'Flying Saucers' with 10cm (4in) wide flowers striped bright blue and white; and 'Heavenly Blue' with beautiful sky-blue flowers.

CULTIVATION
Morning Glory needs a warm sunny sheltered position to succeed outdoors in temperate climates. Provide also a well-drained, fertile soil and a fence or trellis to climb over. A light sandy soil is ideal, and cut off the dead flowers to ensure that more follow.

PROPAGATION
First soak seeds in water for a day to soften the hard seed coat, then sow under glass or indoors during early to mid-spring, one per 7.5cm (3in) pot. Pot on to 12.5cm (5in) pots, harden and plant out when the danger of frost is over.

Lobelia erinus _____
Lobelia

Spread 10cm (4in)
Height 10–20cm (4–8in)

HHA

In Britain Lobelia is in the top-ten list of summer bedding plants, and is widely used in formal bedding, and in containers and hanging baskets. The summers in North American tend to be rather too hot for it to succeed as well.

Lobelia is used as an edging for beds or containers and it goes will with all other summer bedding plants. It is very effective when combined with white Alyssum around the edges of hanging baskets, or planted through the wires. The trailing varieties are best for baskets and edges of other containers.

Lobelia varieties are split into two groups: the compact and the trailing. The main flower colour is blue although there are Lobelias in shades of pink, red and also white. The flowering period is from late spring until the frosts of autumn put a stop to the display. Flowering is continuous and prolific.

Good varieties are 'Blue Stone', a clear blue without a white 'eye', compact habit; 'Cambridge Blue', a true Cambridge blue, compact habit, an extremely popular variety; 'Crystal Palace Compacta', deep blue flowers set against attractive bronze foliage; 'Blue Cascade', trailing variety with Cambridge blue flowers which continue well into the autumn; 'Sapphire', trailing, sapphire-blue flowers each with a white eye; 'String of Pearls', compact variety, includes all the Lobelia colours of blue, violet, rose and white; and 'Colour Cascade', trailing, in a mix which includes blues, reds, mauve, rose-red and white.

CULTIVATION
Lobelia is an adaptable plant and will grow in any type of well-drained soil but it is best in soil which does not dry out excessively in summer, so keep the plants well watered if the soil becomes dry. The best position is in sun although shade for part of the day will not adversely affect growth and flowering.

PROPAGATION
The seeds of Lobelia are as fine as dust and the seedlings tiny, which makes transplanting fiddly. Seeds should be sown under glass or indoors in late winter. Do not cover them with compost. Transplant the seedlings to trays, moving them in batches of three or four, which makes handling so much easier than trying to transplant single seedlings. Grow on in warmth and then harden thoroughly before planting out, which should be done when all danger of frost is over.

Lupinus texensis
Texas Blue Bonnet

Spread 30cm (12in)
Height 30–45cm (12–18in)   **HA**

Myosotis sylvatica (M. oblongata)
Forget-me-not

Spread 15cm (6in)
Height 15–30cm (6–12in)   **HB**

This annual Lupin has spikes of blue flowers, marked with white, in summer and hand-shaped leaves. It is a worthwhile addition to all types of borders and is probably more popular in North America, from where it originates, than in Britain, but it is listed in some British seed catalogues and is worth searching out.

CULTIVATION
A well-drained soil in full sun is needed. Cut off the dead flower heads and watch out for slugs and snails which are partial to the succulent young shoots and leaves.

PROPAGATION
Sow seeds during early spring where the plants are to flower. To aid germination soak the seeds in water for a day before sowing to soften the hard seed coats. The seeds are large enough to sow thinly so, if sown to the correct spacing, there should be no need for subsequent thinning of seedlings.

The Forget-me-not is one of the major subjects for spring bedding schemes and is often planted as a carpet over an entire bed to act as a hazy blue background for tulips. It also combines well with many other spring bedding plants such as Wallflowers, Polyanthus and Winter-flowering Pansies.

It makes a pleasant edging, and is also used in tubs and window boxes, for a spring display with tulips or other spring bulbs.

Varieties of Foreget-me-not include 'Marine', 15cm (6in) high, dwarf and compact with bright mid-blue flowers; 'Royal Blue', 30cm (12in) high, early, with deep indigo-blue flowers; 'Blue Cloud', 30cm (12in) high with true-blue flowers, a less-compact variety ideal for informal planting in a cottage garden; and 'Blue Bird', 30cm (12in) or more in height with long sprays of blue flowers.

The main flowering period is mid-spring to early summer.

CULTIVATION
Forget-me-nots will grow in full sun but they really prefer a position in partial sun – dappled shade cast by trees is ideal. A fertile soil that retains moisture is ideal but it must be well drained. Add bulky organic matter when preparing a bed for For-get-me-nots. Also apply a base dressing of general-purpose fertilizer.

PROPAGATION
Sow seeds in an outdoor seed bed in a spare part of the garden during late spring or early summer. When the seedlings are large enough to handle transplant to nursery rows, spacing them about 15cm (6in) apart each way. Then in early or mid-autumn plant out in their flowering positions.

Nemophila menziesii (N. insignis)
Baby Blue Eyes

Spread 15cm (6in)
Height 15–20cm (6–8in)

HA

Nicandra physalodes
Apple of Peru

Spread 30cm (12in)
Height 90cm (36in)

HA

A charming diminutive hardy annual for the front of borders or for the rock garden. Also try it in gaps in paving, particularly if you have a cottage garden.

The light green feathery foliage makes a nice foil for the small blue, white-eyed bowl-shaped flowers which are produced freely between early and late summer.

CULTIVATION
Any ordinary garden soil is suitable for Baby Blue Eyes provided it drains well. The ideal is a light but moisture-retentive soil to which has been added plenty of compost, peat or leafmould. It will succeed in full sun or partial shade.

PROPAGATION
Seeds are sown in early spring where the plants are to flower and the seedlings thinned out to the recommended distance before they become overcrowded. Alternatively, make a sowing in early autumn for earlier flowering the following year but only if your soil is very well drained.

An unusual hardy annual for any type of border. All its parts are attractive – the leaves, blooms and fruits. It has a branching habit and large wavy-edged leaves. The blooms, which appear between mid-summer and early autumn, are bell-shaped and a pale shade of violet, each having a white throat. Each bloom lasts for only one day. The large inedible fruits which follow are globe-shaped and encased in calyces which are bright green and purple.

CULTIVATION
Full sun is needed for optimum growth together with highly fertile moisture-retentive soil.

PROPAGATION
Although a hardy annual, seeds are best sown under glass or indoors in early spring. Transplant the seedlings to individual 9cm (3½in) pots, and harden well before planting out in late spring.

Nigella damascena
Love-in-a-mist

Spread 20cm (8in)
Height 45–60cm (18–24in)

HA

Phacelia campanularia
Californian Bluebell

Spread 15cm (6in)
Height 22cm (9in)

HA

This is one of the most popular hardy annuals because it's easily grown and makes an excellent show from early to late summer. The bright green feathery foliage makes a nice foil for the blue flowers which are excellent for cutting and arranging indoors. The blooms are followed by large inflated seed pods which are quite attractive and these can be cut and dried for winter flower arrangements. Hang them up for a few weeks in a cool dry airy place. Grow Love-in-a-mist preferably in the annual or mixed border, but it does not look out of place grouped around shrubs. Good varieties are 'Miss Jekyll' with deep sky blue flowers; and 'Persian Jewels' which comes in a mix of colours including light and dark blue, pink and white.

CULTIVATION
Provide a reasonably fertile, well-drained soil in a position which receives plenty of sunshine. Remove the dead flowers to encourage more to follow unless you want to save the seed heads for drying.

PROPAGATION
Sow the seeds in early spring where the plants are to flower and, before the seedlings become overcrowded, thin them to the recommended spacing. In mild areas with well-drained soil, a sowing can be made in early autumn to provide earlier blooms the following year, and it is sensible to overwinter the young plants under cloches.

This easily grown and free-flowering annual is recommended for the front of borders, including shrub and mixed borders. It should be sown in bold groups or it can be selectively sown on rock gardens and in gaps in paving.

The first rich true-blue bell-shaped flowers are produced very soon after germination.

CULTIVATION
Best results are obtained in a sunny spot and a light sandy soil with good drainage. Protect plants from slugs and snails.

PROPAGATION
Sow seeds in early or mid-spring where the plants are to flower and only lightly cover them with fine soil. Before the seedlings become overcrowded, thin them to the recommended spacing. If your garden is in a mild area and the soil drainage is good, a sowing could be made in early autumn. The young plants should be protected during the winter to come earlier into flower the following year.

Salvia farinacea 'Victoria'
Sage

Spread 20–30cm (8–12in)
Height 45cm (18in)   **HHA**

This is an almost hardy perennial but is generally grown as a half-hardy annual. It is a very different type of salvia from *S. splendens,* the Scarlet Sage, and is considered to be one of the finest blue summer bedding plants. Long slender spikes of violet-blue flowers are produced throughout summer until the autumn frosts. This Sage is especially good as a dot plant in summer bedding schemes, especially when combined with plants which have strong colours. It can be used for cutting, and the flowers may be dried for winter decoration if cut as soon as they have opened.

CULTIVATION
Any ordinary soil is suitable as long as the drainage is good and the plant revels in full sun. Cut off dead blooms regularly to encourage more to follow.

PROPAGATION
Sow seeds under glass or indoors during late winter or early spring and transplant seedlings to trays. Harden well and plant out when the danger of frost is over.

Trachelium caeruleum
Throatwort

Spread 30cm (12in)
Height 60–90cm (24–36in)   **HHA**

This is a half-hardy perennial which is generally treated as an annual. It should be grown in a sunny warm border to give blue flowers, which are good for cutting, between early and late summer.

CULTIVATION
It needs a warm, sheltered position in full sun and a light, sandy, well-drained soil. If you do not have the right conditions, you might consider growing it as a pot plant. Cut off the dead flowers, regularly.

PROPAGATION
Sow seeds in early or mid-spring under glass or indoors. Transplant to seed trays, harden well and plant out when the danger of frost is over.

Althaea rosea (A. chinensis)
Annual Hollyhock

Spread 45cm (18in)
Height 60cm–1.8m (2–6ft)

HHA

Antirrhinum majus
Snapdragon

Spread 20–45cm (8–18in)
Height 30–90cm (12–36in)

HHA   S

Hollyhocks are favourite cottage-garden plants flowering from mid-summer to early autumn. They vary from dwarf to typically tall plants and bear their double rounded rosette-like flowers in spikes. The tall varieties are ideal for the back of shrub or mixed borders, and all look good grown against walls or fences. Either side of the front door of a country cottage is still a popular place for these flowers.

Although Hollyhocks are hardy, the annual varieties are given the half-hardy treatment to encourage the plants to flower reasonably early. Varieties include the 60cm (24in) high 'Majorette' which comes in a wide range of colours; and the 1.5–1.8m (5–6ft) high 'Summer Carnival', also in a wide range of colours.

CULTIVATION
Choose a sunny sheltered site. Hollyhocks are not fussy, though they prefer a heavy soil, but high fertility is desirable. Provide supports for tall varieties in exposed gardens, and water freely during dry spells.

PROPAGATION
Sow seeds in late winter under glass or indoors. Transplant to small pots, harden well and plant out in mid-spring. Alternatively sow direct in the flowering site when weather and soil have warmed up sufficiently.

Snapdragons give a superb show from mid-summer on when mass planted. They vary in height from 30cm to 90cm (12–36in) and the dwarf kinds are ideal for planting in large tubs or window boxes.

There are literally dozens of varieties available, with mixtures the most popular though separate colours are available for a colour scheme.

A good tall variety is 'Double Madame Butterfly', 60–75cm (24–30in), with large double blooms in shades of red, pink and yellow. In the intermediate size range – about 45cm (18in) in height – are: 'Coronette' in an excellent mix of colours: and the 'Monarch' series.

An excellent dwarf variety is 'Little Darling', 30cm (12in) high, with open trumpet-shaped flowers in a wide colour range.

CULTIVATION
Snapdragons make few demands: an open, sunny site with reasonably fertile, well-drained soil will suit well. Add bulky organic matter when preparing the soil, and before planting apply a base dressing of general purpose or flower-garden fertilizer.

PROPAGATION
Sow seeds under glass or indoors during late winter or early spring, and cover them only very lightly with fine compost. When seedlings are big enough to handle, transplant to trays and thoroughly harden before planting out in late spring.

Arctotis x hybrida _____
African Daisy

Spread 30cm (12in)
Height 30–60cm (12–24in)   HHA

Begonia × tuberhybrida _____
Tuberous Begonia

Spread 30–38cm (12–15in)
Height 30cm (12in)   HHA

The African Daisy has large daisy-like flowers in many colours from mid-summer until the autumn frosts put a stop to the display. Mass plant them at the front of mixed borders or in formal summer bedding schemes. They are also suitable plants for tubs and window boxes. The blooms are good for cutting and come in many colours: shades of yellow, orange, red, cream and white. Often the blooms are zoned with a contrasting colour. These seeds are only available as large-flowered hybrids.

CULTIVATION
Full sun is needed for optimum flowering together with a well-drained, light soil. Pinch out the tips of young plants when they are about 10cm (4in) high to ensure a bushy habit. Regularly remove dead flowers to encourage more to follow.

PROPAGATION
Sow seeds under glass or indoors during early spring and transplant seedlings to individual 7.5cm (3in) pots. Prererably use a soil-based seed and potting compost. Harden well and plant out when danger of frost is over.

The Tuberous Begonias have long been popular for summer bedding and for containers such as tubs and window boxes and were traditionally grown from tubers. Now it's possible to raise them from seeds. Good seed strains include 'Nonstop', 30cm (12in) high, the best for summer bedding with fully double flowers up to 7.5cm (3in) in diameter which are produced non-stop all summer until the autumn frosts. Colours include shades of red, yellow, pink and also white. 'Clips', 25cm (10in) in height, is new and early flowering, with double blooms in shades of orange, yellow, scarlet and white. Compact and flowering over a long period, 'Clips' is specially recommended for containers such as tubs and window boxes.

CULTIVATION
Grow in full or partial sun in well-drained humus-rich soil. In beds add plenty of peat or leafmould before planting. Regularly cut off dead blooms.

PROPAGATION
Sow seeds under glass or indoors in late winter and do not cover with compost because they are as fine as dust. Transplant to seed trays and grow on in warmth. Before planting out, when all danger of frost is over, harden the plants thoroughly.

Bellis perennis _____
Double Daisy

Spread 15–20cm (6–8in)
Height 15cm (6in)   **HB**

Brassica oleracea capitata _____
Ornamental Cabbage

Spread 30–45cm (12–18in)
Height 30–45cm (12–18in)   **HA HHA**

The varieties of Double Daisies are far superior to the common European daisy, having large fully double flowers in shades of red, pink and white. They are good for spring bedding schemes and achieve a good effect when mass planted. They are also good as a carpet beneath spring tulips or hyacinths. Double Daisies make a fine edging display and again with spring bulbs such as dwarf tulips and hyacinths work well in tubs and window boxes.

The main flowering period is short – mid-spring to early summer, but there are numerous varieties to choose from including the excellent larger flowered 'Goliath' which comes in a mixture of colours; and 'Pomponette' which is also a mixture and produces a profusion of intensely double flowers in rose-pink and white.

How does one incorporate Ornamental Cabbages into flower displays? It is best to use them as dot plants in formal bedding schemes to create extra height and, more importantly, contrast in colour and shape.

Ornamental Cabbages are a good choice for sub-tropical bedding schemes in which they are best planted in bold groups.

Particularly attractive is 'Coral Queen' whose foliage is finely cut and fringed. The centre of the plant becomes red as autumn advances. 'Coral Prince' is the counterpart of 'Coral Queen' but the outer leaves are a lighter green and the centres lemony cream. 'Osaka Red' has brilliant deep mauve-pink heads and the other leaves are dark green. It is also possible to buy Ornamental Cabbages in mixed colours. Also worth growing is Ornamental Kale in mixed colours.

CULTIVATION
Double Daisies will thrive in full or partial sun. They like a fertile garden soil, although any type is suitable provided the drainage is good.

PROPAGATION
Sow the seeds in an outdoor seed bed, in a spare part of the garden, in early summer. Sow in shallow furrows and cover the seeds lightly with fine compost. When the seedlings are large enough to handle transplant them to a nursery bed to grow on. Keep weeded and well watered during the summer. By early or mid-autumn the young plants will be large enough to set out in their flowering positions. Lift carefully and try to retain some soil around the roots.

CULTIVATION
All cabbages like an open sunny position and well-drained fertile soil. So, prepare the ground well by adding plenty of well-rotted manure or compost. Then, before planting, give a dressing of general fertilizer. Chalky or limy soils are generally free or less prone to the cabbage disease, club-root, but it is advisable to treat transplants with club-root dip if your soil is acid.

PROPAGATION
Ornamental Cabbages can be grown as half-hardy or hardy annuals. In the former instance sow under glass or indoors during early spring. Transplant seedlings to individeual 9cm (3½in) pots. Harden off and plant out in late spring.

Alternatively sow outdoors in mid-spring where the plants are to grow or in a nursery bed.

Callistephus chinensis
China Aster

Spread 30cm (12in)
Height 15–90cm (6–36in)

HHA

China Asters are popular for summer colour in mixed borders and for cutting. They have large daisy-like flowers, mostly double, in shades of red, pink, blue, purple and white. Asters are most usually sold as mixtures but separate colours are available. The flowering period is from mid-summer until the autumn frosts arrive. The China Aster is prone to wilt disease so wherever possible buy wilt-resistant varieties and avoid growing the plants in exactly the same spot from year to year.

Recommended varieties include 'Duchess Mixed', 60cm (24in) in height, vigorous well-branched plants with strong stems carrying large double chrysanthemum-like flowers in all the aster colours, which are excellent for cutting. 'Ostrich Feather Mixed' is also highly popular and attains a height of 45cm (18in). The huge fully double blooms have long feathery recurving petals and come in all the usual colours. This variety comes into flower earlier than many.

'Thousand Wonders Mixed' reaches only 15cm (6in) in height and is of bushy habit carrying large double flowers in shades of pink, blue, red and white. 'Thousand Wonders Rose' is the same bushy size and is worth growing for its deep rose-pink blooms.

'Milady Super Mixed' grows to 25cm (10in) and has fully double globular blooms on vigorous sturdy plants in the usual aster colours. If you prefer separate colours try 'Milady Scarlet', 'Milady Rose', 'Milady Blue' and 'Milady White'.

'Powderpuffs' grows to 45–60cm (18–24in) high and has a compact habit of growth. It has large tight double flowers which all open at the same time so the whole plant can be cut if desired and placed in water. Colours in this mix include shades of scarlet, rose, pink, blue, purple and white.

'Totem Pole' is also a mixture of shades and has huge heads of long shaggy petals. Height is 60cm (24in) and is highly recommended for cutting.

CULTIVATION
Grow asters in full sun and fertile soil. Try to find a spot that is sheltered from the wind, especially if growing the taller large-flowered varieties. These may need supporting with short thin canes in windy gardens. Regularly cut off dead flower heads.

PROPAGATION
Sow the seeds under glass or indoors during early spring. Transplant to trays, and thoroughly harden before planting out when the danger of frost is over. Alternatively, seeds can be sown where they are to flower, in mid-spring, and the seedlings thinned to the recommended spacing.

Campanula medium
Canterbury Bells

Spread 30cm (12in)
Height 45–90cm (18–36in)

HB

Canna × generalis
Indian Shot

Spread 30–45cm (12–18in)
Height 60–1205cm (2–4ft)

HHA

Canterbury Bells are delightful old-fashioned plants and a familiar sight in modern as well as cottage gardens, where they are best grown in a mixed border.

Canterbury Bells are sturdy, stong-growing plants flowering between late spring and mid-summer. Popular varieties include 'Cup and Saucer Mixed' which grows to a height of 90cm (36in). The flowers of this mixture do in fact resemble a cup sitting on a saucer. 'Bells of Holland' is a more recent variety and attains a height of 45cm (18in). It's a delightful mixture of pink, blue, mauve and white shades.

Cannas are tender perennials but can be grown from seeds and indeed kept from year to year. The plants have large dramatic foliage in green or purple and exotic-looking flowers in shades of red, orange or yellow. The flowering period is summer. Cannas are often used as dot plants in formal bedding schemes, as centrepieces for large containers and for sub-tropical bedding schemes. Indeed some gardeners regard them as essential plants for the latter. Varieties include 'Giant Hybrids', 60–120cm (2–4ft) and 'Seven Dwarfs', 45cm (18in).

CULTIVATION
Canterbury Bells thrive in full or partial sun and in any ordinary garden soil, provided it is reasonably fertile. It must be well drained, though. Prepare the ground for planting by adding plenty of well-rotted manure or garden compost, and then before planting out apply a base dressing of general purpose or flower garden fertilizer. Guard the plants continuously against slugs and snails, and after the flowers are over the plants can be discarded.

PROPAGATION
Seeds should be sown in mid- to late spring. It is usually best to sow them in a seed tray. Germinate them in a cool greenhouse, cold frame or on a windowsill in a cool room. Transplant the seedlings to trays and, before they become overcrowded, transfer them to a nursery bed in the open, after hardening them. Space them about 15cm (6in) apart in rows. Set out in their flowering positions in early or mid autumn.

CULTIVATION
Cannas grow in any well-drained soil and need a sheltered position in full sun. If you want to keep the plants, lift and dry them off before the frosts start, and overwinter the fleshy rhizomes in a cool but frost-free place.

PROPAGATION
Sow seeds early in the year – before the end of winter. First soak them in water for a day to soften the hard coats and speed up germination. Sow one seed per 7.5cm (3in) pot using peat-based potting compost and germinate in a temperature of 27°C/80°F. Pot on to a 10cm (4in) pot, and thoroughly harden the plants before setting out when the danger of frost is over.

Celosia plumosa _____
Prince of Wales' Feathers

Spread 20–30cm (8–12in)
Height 30–45cm (12–18in)   **HHA**

Centaurea moschata _____
Sweet Sultan

Spread 20cm (8in)
Height 45–60cm (18–24in)   **HA**

In Britain this is generally thought of as a greenhouse pot plant but it can be used for bedding out and is an excellent choice for sub-tropical bedding schemes with its feathery plumes of flowers in shades of mainly red or yellow. It can also be shown effectively in tubs and window boxes.

Good varieties include 'Fairy Fountains', 30cm (12in) high, whose colours include pink, light orange, rich gold and brilliant orange-scarlet. 'Century Mixed', 60cm (24in) high, comes in shades of red and yellow – a really bright mix. 'Apricot Brandy' grows to about 45cm (18in) in height and has beautiful deep bright orange flowers – an unusual colour for celosias.

CULTIVATION
A sheltered spot in full sun is necessary, together with a well-drained soil. Light soil is best but not essential.

PROPAGATION
Sow seeds under glass or indoors during late winter and transplant the seedlings to individual 7.5cm (3in) pots. Pot on to 10–12.5cm (4–5in) pots. Harden thoroughly and plant out when the danger of frost is over.

A delightful old-fashioned annual for mixed borders in cottage, country or even modern town gardens. The large cornflower-shaped flowers are produced from early summer to early autumn and are excellent for cutting. Indeed a row in the vegetable garden specially for this purpose is highly recommended.

Sweet Sultan is sold in a mixture of colours which includes shades of pink, purple and white, and sometimes creamy yellow. 'Giant Imperial Mixed', particularly recommended, grows to a height of 45cm (18in). It has big double flowers in a charming combination of colours.

CULTIVATION
Choose a sunny sheltered position and sow in a fertile well-drained soil. The dead flower heads should be cut off to ensure continuous flowering.

PROPAGATION
Sow seeds where the plants are to flower in early or mid-spring and thin seedlings to the recommended spacing. Further sowings can be made until early summer if desired to ensure a longer flowering season. Also make a sowing in early autumn if you live in a mild area and your soil has impeccable drainage.

Cheiranthus cheiri
Wallflower

Spread 30cm (12in)
Height 30–60cm (12–24in)

HB ☀ **S** ✂ 🌿

In the autumn virtually every garden centre in Britain is stocked with wallflowers, such is the popularity of these spring bedding plants. They are not so widely planted in America because the winters are generally too cold for them. Indeed, a severe winter in the UK can result in considerable losses, so be prepared for this. Nevertheless this does not deter gardeners from planting wallfowers in their millions.

Certainly they make a marvellous show in the period from early spring to early summer. Flowers come in a wide range of colours – shades of red, scarlet, crimson, purple, pink, yellow, orange, cream, white, etc. Most popular are the mixtures of colours, but separate colours are also available.

Wallflowers are generally mass planted in formal beds, or bold groups planted at the front of mixed borders, often with tall tulips growing through them. They associate well with other spring bedding plants such as Forget-me-nots, Polyanthus, Double Daisies and Winter-flowering Pansies.

Among the many varieties that can be recommended is 'Fair Lady Mixed', 50cm (20in) high, which has a compact habit and all the usual wallflower colours, plus pastel shades.

The 'Bedder' series is highly recommended. The plants are dwarf, about 30cm (12in) in height, and ideal for mass planting in formal beds. You can buy a mixture, or separate colours: 'Orange Bedder', rich orange and apricot; 'Scarlet Bedder', deep, bright, rich scarlet; 'Golden Bedder', large early golden-yellow blooms; and 'Primrose bedder', primrose-yellow.

Try also the Siberian Wallflower, *Cheiranthus allionii*. It is dwarf, at 30cm (12in) high, compact, free flowering and has bright orange blooms. Varieties are 'Orange Bedder', bright orange; 'Golden Bedder', golden-yellow; and 'Yellow Bedder', pure yellow.

CULTIVATION
The soil must be well drained because if it lies wet over winter the plants are liable to die. However, any soil type is suitable for Wallflowers and they do particularly well on chalky or limy soils. Apply lime to acid soils. Full sun is needed, and shelter from cold winter winds. Sometimes hard frosts partially lift the plants out of the ground and if this happens they must be refirmed immediately or again they could die. For the sake of

PROPAGATION
Sow seeds in an outdoor seed bed during late spring or early summer. Then transplant the seedlings to a nursery bed, spacing them about 20cm (8in) apart each way. Keep weeded and water well during dry spells. It pays to treat roots of wallflowers with a proprietary clubroot dip to prevent this serious disease from crippling the plants. Wallflowers are planted in their flowering positions during mid-autumn – lift them with some soil around the roots if possible because then they re-establish more quickly.

Chrysanthemum carinatum (C. tricolor) _____
Annual Chrysanthemum

Spread 30cm (12in)
Height 60cm (24in)

HA

Cucurbita pepo ovifera _____
Ornamental Gourd

Spread 90cm (36in)
Height up to 3m (10ft)

HHA

An easily grown and popular hardy annual, especially good for cutting because the blooms last well in water. The large daisy flowers are produced from early summer to early autumn. Sold in a mix of colours which includes shades of orange, yellow, red and also white. The flowers are zoned with a contrasting colour.

Also recommended is *C. multicaule* 'Gold Plate', a low grower at 15cm (6in) high, with a spreading habit and golden-yellow flowers – ideal for containers such as tubs and window boxes. Try also *C. paludosum*, 30cm (12in) high, with masses of small white and yellow flowers with yellow centres all summer, useful for containers and for edging beds.

CULTIVATION
Well-drained soil in full sun is needed for best results. Regularly remove dead flowers to ensure more to follow. Tall kinds may need twiggy sticks for support in windy gardens.

PROPAGATION
Sow seeds in early or mid-spring where the plants are to flower and thin out the seedlings to the recommended spacing. Or make a sowing in early autumn if you have well-drained soil and live in a mild area. Cover plants with cloches for the winter.

Ornamental Gourds are grown for their fruits, which vary tremendously in shape, size and colours. The fruits are dried and used for winter decoration indoors.

There are several varieties including 'Small Fruited Mixed' with fruits in all shapes and colours.

CULTIVATION
Gourds are climbers and should be trained up suitable supports such as walls or fences equipped with trellis panels. Or grow the plants up a tripod of canes or sticks. The plants need full sun, a sheltered spot and a well-drained soil.

The fruits are cut in the autumn and kept for a few weeks in a warm dry place to allow them to dry out. They they can be varnished to give them a shine.

PROPAGATION
Sow seeds under glass or indoors during late spring, one seed per 9cm (3½in) pot. Harden thoroughly and plant out when the danger of frost is over.

Dahlia variabilis
Dahlia

Spread 30–60cm (12–24in)
Height 30–60cm (12–24in)

HHA

Dwarf Bedding Dahlias are easily raised from seeds and make a superb show from early or mid-summer until the frosts put a stop to the display. Flowering is continuous throughout the season.

Dahlias are stricly tender perennials but the bedding kinds are generally treated as half-hardy annuals. The flowers come in a wide range of colours and are excellent for cutting.

Dahlias can be used in various ways: they can be mass planted in beds, planted in bold groups in mixed borders, used as dot plants in formal bedding schemes, included in sub-tropical bedding schemes and planted in tubs or window boxes.

There are lots of dwarf varieties available including 'Unwins Dwarf Hybrids', 45–60cm (18–24in) in height, highly popular on both sides of the Atlantic, with semi-double blooms in a vast range of colours. Flowers are freely produced on bushy plants. Plants will start flowering in three months from sowing.

'Coltness Hybrids', 45cm (18in) high, are also well-known, having single flowers in a wide range of colours, freely produced on compact plants.

'Redskin', 30cm (12in) high, has gained many awards in trials, has double flowers in a range of colours, and bronze-green to maroon foliage. 'Rigoletto', 30cm (12in) high, comes into flower early, the compact plants carrying masses of double blooms in a wide range of colours. One of the best for mass bedding.

CULTIVATION
Full sun is essential for optimum flowering. Provide, too, a fertile soil although any soil is suitable. Prepare it by adding plenty of bulky organic matter such as well-rotted farmyard manure or garden compost. Apply a base dressing of general-purpose or flower-garden fertilizer before planting. Protect plants from slugs and snails by using slug pellets. Water well during dry periods in summer and give a liquid feed monthly to established plants. Regularly cut off dead flowers to ensure that plenty more follow.

PROPAGATION
Sow seeds under glass or indoors during late winter. Transplant seedlings to individual 9cm (3½in) pots. Harden thoroughly and plant out when the danger of frost is over.

Delphinium consolida _____
Larkspur

Spread 30cm (12in)
Height 30–120cm (12–48in)   HA  S

A highly popular and easily grown hardy annual that makes a fine show in annual or mixed borders between early and late summer. Makes an ideal cut-flower, too. Flowers come in various colours: pink, red, purple, blue and white. Sold as mixtures such as 'Giant Imperial', up to 120cm (48in) in height, with a branching habit and long spikes of double blooms in pink, blue and white. 'Dwarf Hyacinth-Flowered' Double Mixed' grows to only 30cm (12in) in height and the compact plants have blooms in shades of pink, blue and white.

Also worth growing is another annual delphinium, *D. chinensis* 'Blue Mirror', 30cm (12in) in height with large gentian-blue flowers. It's best grown as a half-hardy annual.

Dianthus barbatus _____
Sweet William

Spread 20cm (8in)
Height 30–60cm (12–24in)   HB

No self-respecting cottage garden should be without Sweet Williams. They were seen in most cottage gardens of the past and are still as popular as ever. In modern gardens they fit into the mixed border, associating well with herbaceous perennials, especially early-summer flowering kinds such as lupins, irises, peonies and Oriental poppies.

The flowering period of Sweet Williams is early to mid-summer. Colours include shades of red, pink and also white. Sweet Williams are generally sold in mixtures of colours, such as 'Extra Dwarf Double Mixed', 30cm (12in) high compact plants with mainly double flowers in bright and cheerful colours. 'Auricula-eyed Mixed' is the old-fashioned sort, each flower having a contrasting centre.

CULTIVATION
Larkspur grows in any ordinary well-drained soil and full sun. The tall varieties will need twiggy sticks to support the slender stems.

PROPAGATION
Sow sees where the plants are to flower, in early or mid-spring and thin out the seedlings before they become overcrowded. Alternatively make a sowing in early autumn if you live in a mild area and have well-drained soil. Cover young plants with cloches for the winter, if available. Guard against slugs and snails.

CULTIVATION
Sweet Williams need full sun for optimum flowering, and a well-drained soil, which must be well prepared before planting by adding bulky organic matter. Apply a base dressing of general purpose fertilizer before planting, and guard the plants against slugs and snails.

PROPAGATION
Seeds are sown in early summer in a well-prepared seed bed in a spare part of the garden. As soon as the seedlings are large enough to handle they should be transplanted to a nursery bed to grow on. Space them about 20cm (8in) apart each way. The young plants are set out in their flowering positions in early or mid-autumn, and they should be lifted with some soil around the roots if possible to ensure that they re-establish quickly.

Echium plantagineum (E. lycopsis)
Viper's Bugloss

Spread 45cm (18in)
Height 30–90cm (12–36in)

HA

Gaillardia pulchella
Blanket Flower

Spread 30cm (12in)
Height 45–60cm (18–24in)

HA

A good but possibly not too well-known hardy annual for the annual or mixed border. It's a bushy plant up to 90cm (36in) high in the species with bluish or purplish flowers carried in spikes during early to late summer. However, hybrids are normally grown which come in mixtures of colours: 'Dwarf Hybrids' are especially recommended, growing to about 30cm (12in) in height, in a mix of colours that includes blue and pink shades, mauve and white. The dwarf ones would also be suitable for growing in tubs and window boxes.

Colourful daisy-flowered annual which makes a brilliant show between mid-summer and mid-autumn. The blooms are large and excellent for cutting. There are several varieties but 'Double Mixed' is popular, with double blooms in a range of colours that includes red, gold, cream and bi-colours.

Grow Gaillardias in the annual or mixed border.

CULTIVATION
Any ordinary garden soil is suitable for the Viper's Bugloss provided it is well drained. The plant actually prefers a dry light soil. Full sun is necessary for optimum flowering.

PROPAGATION
Seeds are sown where they are to flower in early spring and the seedlings thinned to the recommended spacing. Alternatively, if your soil is very light and well drained make a sowing in early autumn and overwinter the young plants under cloches. You will then get earlier blooms the following year.

CULTIVATION
A sunny site is needed but any well-drained soil is suitable. A light sandy soil is preferred but is not essential. A few twiggy sticks may be needed for support. Regularly cut off dead flower heads, when more blooms will follow.

PROPAGATION
Sow seeds where the plants are to flower, in mid-spring, and thin out the seedlings to the recommended distance. Alternatively, if you want earlier blooms, make a sowing under glass or indoors during late winter or early spring, transplant seedlings to trays, harden thoroughly and plant out in late spring.

Gazania × hybrida _____
Treasure Flower

Spread 30cm (12in)
Height 20–30cm (8–12in)   HHA

The low-growing Treasure Flowers are sun-worshippers and recommended for a hot dry site. Most have deep green or greyish foliage and large daisy flowers in shades of yellow, orange, mahogany, red, pink and cream, which usually open only in bright weather. Mainly used for edging, planted in bold drifts and to fill tubs and window boxes, they will also provide colour on the rock garden. They flower from mid-summer until the first frosts.

Latest varieties include 'Mini-star Tangerine' and 'Mini-star Yellow' with flowers more inclined to stay open in dull weather; 'Mini-star Mixed' contains a wide range of colours; 'Sundance' has exceptionally large flowers in a mixture of colours that includes red and yellow stripes, crimson, purple, orange, yellow and cream; and 'Daybreak' flowers stay open even longer in dull weather.

CULTIVATION
A position in full sun is essential together with a well-drained soil. Any soil type is, however, suitable.

If in a wet summer any blooms are affected by grey mould fungus (botrytis) cut these off to prevent the disease from spreading.

PROPAGATION
Sow seeds under glass or indoors during late winter. Transplant seedlings to individual 7.5cm (3in) pots and make sure they are well hardened before planting out, which should be done when the danger of frost is over.

Helichrysum bracteatum _____
Strawflower

Spread 30cm (12in)
Height 30–90cm (12–36in)   HHA

The Strawflower has double daisy-like flowers with a straw-like texture in shades of red, pink, yellow, orange and white. It is grown mainly for cutting and drying for winter decoration although the plants make an attractive show in the annual or mixed border.

The Strawflower is available as mixtures including 'Double Mixed', 90cm (36in) high; 'Bright Bikinis', 30–38cm (12–15in) high, in a wide range of bright colours; and 'Hot Bikini', 30–38cm (12–15in) high, with rich red flowers.

CULTIVATION
Provide a spot in full sun and a very well drained soil. Strawflowers do not mind light poor soils and indeed in such conditions the flower colour is more intense. Flowers for drying should be cut before they are completely open (before the disc in the centre shows), loosely bundled and hung upside down in a cool dry airy place away from direct sun. They will be thoroughly dry in a few weeks.

PROPAGATION
Sow seeds under glass or indoors during late winter/early spring. Transplant to trays, harden thoroughly and plant out in late spring when the danger of frost is over.

Lathyrus odoratus
Sweet Pea

Spread 15–20cm (6–8in)
Height 30cm (12in) to 3m (10ft)

HA ☀ **S** ✂ 🌿

Sweet Peas are highly popular in Britain but of only minor interest in the USA. Many varieties have highly fragrant flowers and are excellent for cutting. They make a good show in annual or mixed borders. Some are dwarf bushy plants, others tall, ideal for growing up trellis, walls, fences and wigwams of tall twiggy sticks or bamboo canes.

There is an enormously wide range of varieties to choose from and the flowers come in virtually every colour. Mixtures as well as separate colours are available.

All we can do here is to describe a representative selection of varieties, both tall and dwarf.

'Early Mammoth Mixed' is a tall multiflora type that is noted for early flowering, large, long-stemmed blooms and fragrance. 'Early Wonder Mixed' is also a tall climber that comes into bloom early and has good fragrance. 'Galaxy Mixed', tall, comes in a wide range of beautiful colours and has many flowers on each stem. Probably better known in Britain than in North America are the Spencer varieties, which are tall climbers and popular for cutting. There are dozens of named varieties in separate colours.

Among the dwarf varieties, highly recommended is 'Jet Set Mixed', about 90cm (36in) in height, with large flowers on long stems and up to seven blooms per stem. 'Knee-Hi' mixed is virtually identical.

'Snoopea Mixed' does not have tendrils on the leaves. It cannot climb, so it forms a sort of annual ground cover about 30cm (12in) in height and freely produces normal-sized blooms on long stems. 'Supersnoop Mixed' is really an improved 'Snoopea' but it comes into flower up to 10 days earlier. The flower stems are longer and there is a wider range of colours. Last but not least is 'Bijou Mixed',

which grows only 30–38cm (12–15in) high and wide. Despite its diminutive size the blooms are large and each stem carries up to five flowers.

The flowering period of Sweet Peas is early summer to early autumn.

CULTIVATION
An open sunny site is needed with a well-drained fertile soil, well-enriched with manure or compost and fertilizer. Water well in summer, liquid feed fortnightly and remove dead flowers. Pinch out growing tips of seedlings when 10cm (4in) high. Protect from slugs and snails.

PROPAGATION
Soak seeds in water for half a day before sowing. Sow in early or mid-spring in trays and germinate in a cold frame or indoors in a cool room. Do not allow them to become too damp during germination. Plant out in late spring. Alternatively sow seeds where they are to flower during early or mid-spring.

Limonium sinuatum (Statice sinuata)
Sea Lavender

Spread 30cm (12in)
Height 45cm (18in)

HHA

Linaria maroccana
Toadflax

Spread 15cm (6in)
Height 20–30cm (8–12in)

HA

Sea Lavender is grown mainly for cutting and drying for winter flower arrangements but the sprays of flowers also make a fine show in the annual or mixed border.

Usually available in mixtures of colours including shades of blue, red, pink, yellow, etc. 'Mixed Hybrids' is a good mix of pastel colours. 'Blue River' is compact and has blue flowers. The flowering period is mid-summer to early autumn.

CULTIVATION
An open position in full sun is recommended. Any well-drained soil is suitable. Flowers should be cut for drying just before they are completely open. Bundle loosely and hang them upside down for a few weeks in a cool dry airy place out of direct sun.

PROPAGATION
Sow seeds under glass or indoors during late winter/early spring. Transplant the seedlings to trays, harden thoroughly and plant out in late spring.

Popular and easily grown hardy annual used for edging beds and borders, for sowing in gaps in paving and for providing colour on the rock garden. Every cottage garden should have some!

The little antirrhinum-like flowers come in a wide range of colours and the flowering period is early and mid-summer.

Sold as mixtures, particularly recommended is 'Fairy Bouquet' in a wide range of colours and attaining about 20cm (8in) in height.

CULTIVATION
For best results grow Toadflax in full sun and well-drained soil.

PROPAGATION
Sow the seeds during early or mid-spring where the plants are to flower, and before overcrowding occurs thin the seedlings to the recommended spacing. A sowing can also be made outdoors in early autumn to provide earlier blooms the following year. Only suitable for well-drained soils. Cover with cloches over winter if you live in a cold area.

Matthiola incana _____
Stock

Spread 30cm (12in)
Height 30–60cm (12–24in) **HA HHA HB** S ✂

Stocks, annual and biennial, are best loved for their scented flowers.

Among the annual stocks are the selectable 'Park Stocks' (HHA) 30cm (12in) in a mix of colours. To ensure you get double-flowers, grow seedlings at 5–7°C (40–45°F) for several days and then select only light green ones (double-flowered). 'Large Flowering Ten Week Mixed' (HHA) 30cm (12in) has a fine range of colours and compact habit. 'Giant Excelsior' column stocks (HHA) reach 60cm (24in), and are fine for cutting. *Matthiola bicornis*, the Night-scented Stock (HA) reaches 30cm (12in) with pale lilac flowers.

The Brompton Stocks are hardy biennials 60cm (24in) and give fine spring colour.

CULTIVATION
Stocks will thrive in full or partial sun but need a well-drained fertile soil.

PROPAGATION
Sow hardy annual kinds during early to mid-spring where the plants are to flower and thin to the recommended spacing. Those treated as half-hardy annuals are sown under glass or indoors during late winter/early spring. Sow biennial stocks in an outdoor seed bed during late spring/early summer. Transplant seedlings to a nursery bed and plant out young plants in their flowering positions during mid-autumn. Protect with cloches over winter in windy gardens.

Mesembryanthemum criniflorum _____
Livingstone Daisy

Spread 30cm (12in)
Height 15cm (6in) **HHA**

A popular little annual with masses of daisy flowers in a wide range of bright colours. These open only when the sun is shining or during bright weather. They are ideal for hot dry places such as banks, the rock garden and for gaps in paving. The flowering period is early to late summer.

Another Livingstone Daisy worth growing is *M. oculatum* 'Yellow Lunette', with early bright yellow flowers which open in duller conditions.

CULTIVATION
A hot dry spot is essential for success. Light poor sandy soils are ideal. Watch out for slugs and snails because they are partial to the soft succulent leaves and stems.

PROPAGATION
Seeds are sown under glass or indoors during early spring and the seedlings transplanted to trays. Harden thoroughly and plant out when the danger of frost is over. Alternatively, a sowing can be made during mid-spring where the plants are to flower and the resultant seedlings thinned to the recommended spacing.

Mimulus × hybridus
Monkey Flower

Spread 20–30cm (8–12in)
Height 15–20cm (6–8in)   **HHA**

In recent years mimulus have become popular for bedding out. Possibly this is because some exciting new hybrids such as 'Calypso' have been introduced with flowers in shades of red, pink, orange and yellow, some being bi-coloured; and 'Malibu' with rich deep orange blooms.

Mimulus can be mass planted in beds and are excellent for containers such as tubs, window boxes and hanging baskets. They have numerous flushes of blooms throughout the summer and can start flowering in as little as seven or eight weeks from sowing.

CULTIVATION
In temperate climates mimulus will succeed in full sun, and in partial shade. In hot climates, though, plant them in shade. The soil must be able to retain moisture during the summer because mimulus thrive in moist conditions. Add plenty of bulky organic matter especially if the soil is light and sandy.

Cut off dead flower heads to encourage more blooms to follow, and guard against slugs and snails especially after planting.

PROPAGATION
Sow seeds under glass or indoors during early or mid-spring and transplant the resultant seedlings to trays. Make sure you don't allow the compost to dry out at any time. Harden thoroughly before planting out in late spring. The plants are short-lived perennials but are normally treated as annuals and discarded at the end of the season.

Mirabilis jalapa
Four O'Clock Plant

Spread 30cm (12in)
Height 60cm (24in)   **HHA**   **S**

The Four O'Clock Plant is a colourful perennial which is grown as an annual in the annual or mixed border. The scented blooms are trumpet-shaped and come in various shades including red, pink, yellow and white. They open in late afternoon, hence the common name, and by the following morning are over, but plenty more follow – indeed this is a free-flowering annual. The blooms may open earlier in the day during dull or cool weather. The Four O'Clock Plant flowers from mid-summer to early autumn.

CULTIVATION
Provide a spot in full sun and sheltered from winds. The plant prefers a light soil but whichever type you have it should be moderately fertile for best growth and flowering. In windy gardens twiggy sticks may have to be provided to support the plants.

PROPAGATION
Sow the seeds under glass or indoors during late winter or early spring. The seedlings are transplanted to trays, thoroughly hardened and planted out when the danger of frost is over.

Nemesia strumosa
Nemesia

Spread 10–15cm (4–6in)
Height 20–45cm (8–18in)

HHA

A popular half-hardy annual suitable for bedding out in formal beds, for planting in bold groups at the front of a mixed border and for growing specially for cutting.

It's a bushy upright plant producing tubular flowers from early to late summer. Varieties come in mixtures of colours including shades of red, pink, orange, yellow and cream. Good varieties are 'Carnival Mixed', 20–30cm (8–12in) high; 'Funfair', 20cm (8in), an exceedingly bright and warm mix of colours; and 'Triumph Mixed' ('Dwarf Compact Hybrids'), 20cm (8in), with bright showy colours and a compact habit.

CULTIVATION
Grow in full or partial sun and any ordinary soil well supplied with bulky organic matter. The plant actually prefers a light sandy acid or lime-free soil but these conditions are not essential. Keep well watered in dry weather because dry conditions lead to poor growth and flowering. Cut off dead flowers to ensure that more follow.

PROPAGATION
Sow seeds under glass or indoors during early spring, transplant seedlings to trays, harden thoroughly and plant out when the danger of frost is over.

Nicotiana alata (N. affinis)
Ornamental Tobacco

Spread 30cm (12in)
Height 30–90cm (12–36in)

HHA

Ornamental Tobacco is a lovely summer bedding plant, producing a wealth of colourful, often scented flowers from early summer to early autumn.

Grow nicotiana in formal displays, for planting in bold groups in borders, and in containers, especially the shorter varieties.

Good varieties include 'Nicki Formula Mixed', 38cm (15in) high, which is sweetly scented. 'Senation Mixed', 75–90cm (30–36in) high, is also scented and unlike some varieties the flowers open during the day rather than in the evening, as do those of 'Domino Mixed', 30cm (12in) high, in a good range of colours including bi-colours on bushy plants.

It is also possible to buy varieties in separate colours. There are separate colours in the 'Domino' and 'Nicki' series. Probably the most popular single-coloured nicotiana is 'Lime Green' 60cm (24in) in height with greenish yellow flowers.

CULTIVATION
Best results are achieved in a sunny sheltered spot. Nicotiana likes a fertile soil, so prepare the ground well by adding plenty of well-rotted manure or garden compost. Before planting give a base dressing of fertilizer.

PROPAGATION
Sow seeds under glass or indoors during late winter or early spring. Do not cover them with compost. Transplant seedlings to trays, or to 9cm (3½in) pots if preferred, harden thoroughly and plant out when the danger of frost is over.

Papaver nudicaule _____
Iceland Poppy

Spread 30cm (12in)
Height 45–76cm (18–30in)   **HHA HB**

Papaver rhoeas _____
Field Poppy or Shirley Poppy

Spread 30cm (12in)
Height 76–90cm (30–36in)   **HA**

The Iceland Poppy can be grown either as a half-hardy annual or as a biennial. Strictly speaking it is a short-lived perennial. The flowers are suitable for cutting and a bold group of plants makes a fine show in an annual or mixed border during the summer. The foliage is lobed and light green, a nice background for the large flowers which come in many colours.

Varieties include 'Unwins Giant Coonara', 45cm (18in) high, a mix of bright and pastel colours; 'Champagne Bubbles', 45–60cm (18–24in) high, wide range of colours including shades of red, yellow, pink, orange and white; and 'Oregon Rainbows', height up to 45cm (18in) with strong stems ideal for cutting and flowers in shades of orange, pink, yellow, cream, etc.

CULTIVATION
Any well-drained soil in full sun will do. Remove dead blooms. Flowers for arranging should be cut just as they are opening and the stem bases dipped in hot water to seal them.

PROPAGATION
To grow as a half-hardy annual sow under glass or indoors in late winter, transplant to small pots, harden and plant out in late spring. To grow as a biennial sow outdoors where the plants are to flower during late spring and thin out the seedlings. Cover with cloches over winter.

The species, which is shown above, is not often grown in gardens but rather the varieties, particularly 'Shirley Double Mixed' with double blooms in shades of red, pink, white, etc. These are produced between early and late summer and make a bright colourful show in the annual or mixed border.

CULTIVATION
Any ordinary well-drained soil in full sun will enable Field Poppies to be grown. Dead flowers should be removed regularly.

PROPAGATION
Sow seeds where the plants are to flower during early or mid-spring and thin out the seedlings to the recommended spacing.

Papaver somniferum
Opium Poppy

Spread 30cm (12in)
Height 76–90cm (30–36in)   HA

The species has quite attractive pale grey-green lobed leaves, a pleasant contrast to the red, pink, purple or white flowers that are produced from early to late summer. But varieties are usually grown in gardens, particularly 'Paeony-flowered Mixed' with fully double globular flowers in a good mix of colours including shades of pink and red.

The Opium Poppy is best sown in bold groups in the mixed or annual border.

CULTIVATION
Provide a well-drained soil in full sun for best results. Fairly poor soils are suitable, too. Regularly cut off dead flowers.

PROPAGATION
Sow seeds where the plants are to flower during early or mid-spring and thin out the seedlings to the recommended spacing before they start to become overcrowded.

Pelargonium peltatum
Ive-leaf Geranium

Spread 30cm (12in)
Height 30cm (12in)   HHA

The Ivy-leaf Geranium is popular for summer bedding, for mass planting in formal beds, and for containers such as tubs, urns, window boxes and hanging baskets, flowering continuously from early summer until the autumn frosts. Colours include shades of red, pink and also white.

Prior to the recent introduction of seed-raised varieties one had to buy young plants or raise new ones from cuttings taken in late summer.

The flowers of the F1 hybrid 'Summer Showers' are pink, mauve, red and also white. Completely trailing, the plants are ideal for hanging baskets and window boxes. Plants start coming into flower some 17–18 weeks from sowing and they make a magnificent display.

CULTIVATION
Provide a position in full sun to encourage optimum flowering. Any well-drained soil is suitable if you are planting in beds, provided it is reasonably fertile. If growing in containers use a good-quality potting compost, either soil-based or soilless (peat-based).

PROPAGATION
Seeds must be sown early in the year – mid-winter is recommended if you want plants in flower by early summer. Seeds can be sown under glass or indoors in adequate warmth. Seedlings are transplanted to 7.5cm (3in) pots and if necessary potted on to 12.5cm (5in) pots. Harden well and plant out when the danger of frost is over.

Petunia × hybrida
Petunia

Spread 30cm (12in)
Height 15–38cm (6–15in)

HHA

Petunias are in the top-ten list of summer bedding plants, being used extensively for mass-planting in formal beds with other half-hardy annuals, and in containers such as tubs, urns, window boxes and hanging baskets. Most petunias are bushy plants but some varieties have a somewhat trailing habit and these are especially useful for containers, although the bushy ones are also suitable.

Petunias come in an enormously wide range of colours, in mixtures and separate colours. The flowers are trumpet-shaped and some varieties have double blooms. The flowering period is early summer to autumn when the frosts put a stop to the display.

There are several groups of petunias, including the multiflora varieties which are the best types for bedding, being bushy plants with masses of small flowers. Varieties include the 'Resisto' series, free flowering, the blooms standing up well to wet weather. There is 'Resisto Mixed' in a blend of bright colours; 'Resisto Blue', a beautiful mid-blue; and 'Resisto Rose-pink', the colour being as the name. The 'Jamboree' series is also recommended. Particularly popular is 'Jamboree Mixed' with exceptionally large flowers for a multiflora type, especially recommended for hanging baskets and window boxes as well as for bedding. The 'Madness' series – officially a floribunda – has flowers approaching grandiflora size, with compact habit, but flowers as freely as multiflora types.

The grandiflora petunias are giant-flowered varieties and are especially recommended for tubs and window boxes but are also impressive in beds. They are not quite so weather-resistant as the multifloras – blooms can be marked by rain. The 'Picotee' series is highly recommended,

including 'Red Picotee' in bright scarlet with a broad white picotee edge, and 'Blue Frost' in deep violet-blue with a pure white edge. The 'Flash' series is popular in America for its early flowering and uniform habit with many bright colours.

CULTIVATION
Best flowering achieved in full sun but partial sun is also suitable. Any well-drained soil gives good results as long as it's reasonably fertile. But it must not be too rich, or the plants will make vegetative growth at the expense of flowers. A sheltered site is recommended for the grandiflora petunias. Regularly remove dead flower heads and guard the plants against slugs and snails.

PROPAGATION
Sow seed as under glass or indoors during early spring. The seeds are minute so do not cover them with compost. Transplant seedlings to trays, harden thoroughly and plant out when the danger of frost is over.

Phlox drummondii
Annual Phlox

Spread 20cm (8in)
Height 15–30cm (6–12in)

 **HHA**

Portulaca grandiflora
Sun Plant

Spread 15cm (6in)
Height 15cm (6in)

 HHA

Annual Phlox is a bright colourful little plant suitable for mass planting in beds, edging, containers and even for providing colour on the rock garden. It flowers from mid-summer to early autumn and colours include shades of red, pink, purple and white.

Annual Phlox is sold as mixtures of colours and include 'Twinkle Dwarf Star Mixed', 15cm (6in) high, with masses of dainty star-like blooms; and 'Beauty Formula Mixed', 30cm (12in) high, a mixture of brilliantly coloured varieties without the usual contrasting centres.

The Sun Plant is a succulent with fleshy stems and leaves and bears brilliant flowers in shades of red, pink, yellow, etc, from early summer to early autumn. It is an ideal plant for a hot dry bank, the rock garden or for edging beds and borders.

A good variety is 'Sunnyside' Mixed', with large rose-like double blooms in a mix of 12 bright clear colours.

CULTIVATION
Grow Annual Phlox in any reasonably fertile well-drained soil in full sun. The removal of dead flower heads will ensure more blooms to follow. Guard against slugs and snails.

PROPAGATION
Sow seeds under glass or indoors during early spring, transplant the seedlings to trays, harden thoroughly and plant out when the danger of frost is over. Or, sow outdoors in mid spring where the plants are to flower.

CULTIVATION
Full sun is essential together with good drainage – plants thrive in hot dry conditions. There is no need to water in a dry summer unless the plants are obviously flagging. Regularly remove dead flower heads.

PROPAGATION
Sow seeds under glass or indoors during early spring, transplant seedlings to trays, harden well and plant out when the danger of frost is over. Alternatively, sow outdoors during late spring where the plants are to flower and thin out the seedlings to the recommended spacing.

Primula polyantha _____
Polyanthus

Spread 20cm (8in)
Height 15–22cm (6–9in)

HB

Salvia horminum _____
Clary

Spread 20cm (8in)
Height 45–60cm (18–24in)

HA

In Britain, Polyanthus are widely grown as spring bedding plants in formal beds and in containers such as tubs and window boxes. In N. America they are grown as pot plants.

Plant them in beds, on their own or with spring bulbs such as dwarf tulips and hyacinths. They bloom over several months in the spring. Plant them in mixed borders or drift them around spring-flowering shrubs in a shrub border.

Some recommended varieties include 'Pacific Giants Mixed', with large blooms in bright colours, and 'Pacific Giants Blue Shades' in various shades of blue – these really need some protection in winter; and 'Crescendo', again with large flowers on vigorous hardy plants, the brilliant colour range including shades of yellow, red and pink.

CULTIVATION
Polyanthus prefer dappled shade cast by trees, and ordinary garden soil as long as it is moisture retentive (though not wet or waterlogged in winter). Add plenty of peat or leafmould to light sandy or chalky soil to help retain moisture. Before planting apply a base dressing of fertilizer. And fill tubs and window boxes with soilless (peat-based) potting compost.

PROPAGATION
Sow seeds in late spring and take care the temperature stays below 18°C/65°F. Transplanted seedlings should be kept cool and shaded in the trays and later in a nursery bed. Plant in final positions in early to mid-autumn.

This easily grown hardy annual makes a fine show in the annual or mixed border from early summer to early autumn. The flower bracts come in various colours such as red, pink, purple, blue and white. The blooms are excellent for cutting and can even be dried for winter decoration.

Good varieties include 'Art Shades', 60cm (24in) high, in shades of pink, rose, blue and white; 'Claryssa', 45cm (18in), a new variety in a wide range of bright colours; 'Claryssa Blue', 'Claryssa Pink' and 'Claryssa White'.

CULTIVATION
Any well-drained soil in full sun gives good results. Regularly cut off dead flower heads to encourage more to follow.

PROPAGATION
Sow seeds in their flowering positions during early to mid-spring and before the seedlings become overcrowded thin them out to the recommended spacing.

Scabiosa atropurpurea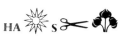
Sweet Scabious

Spread 20cm (8in)
Height 45–90cm (18–36in)

HA ☀ S ✂ 🌸

This is an excellent annual for cutting and for providing colour in annual or mixed borders from mid-summer to early autumn. Varieties are usually grown, such as 'Double Mixed', 90cm (36in) high with double scented blooms in shades of blue, purple, red, pink and white; and 'Dwarf Double Mixed', 45cm (18in) high in a similar colour range with fully double scented flowers.

CULTIVATION
Full sun, any fertile well-drained soil is needed for optimum flowering. Watch out for slugs and snails, which are rather partial to Sweet Scabious. Regularly remove dead flower heads to encourage more blooms to follow. Tall varieties may need a few twiggy sticks for support.

PROPAGATION
Sow seeds where the plants are to flower during early or mid-spring and thin the resultant seedlings. Alternatively, make a sowing in early autumn for earlier blooms the following spring and cover the young plants with cloches over winter if you live in a cold area.

Schizanthus pinnatus
Poor Man's Orchid

Spread 30cm (12in)
Height 15–45cm (6–18in)

HHA ☀ ✂ 🌸

The Poor Man's Orchid is generally grown as a greenhouse pot plant but it can be bedded out for the summer provided a sunny sheltered spot is chosen. As well as for mass planting in beds, it is also an ideal subject for window boxes and tubs.

It's a bushy plant with ferny foliage, which produces a profusion of multi-coloured flowers between early summer and the autumn.

Most varieties these days are dwarf or comparatively low-growing, such as 'Disco', 30cm (12in) high; 'Hit Parade', 30cm (12in), in a mix of rich and beautiful colours; and 'Star Parade', 15–20cm (6–8in), excellent for mass planting.

CULTIVATION
Choose a sheltered spot in full sun, and a well-drained soil. The plants prefer a light sandy soil which should be improved with bulky organic matter such as peat. Provide twiggy sticks to support the taller varieties.

PROPAGATION
Sow seeds under glass or indoors during early spring and transplant seedlings to small pots. Harden thoroughly and plant outdoors when the danger of frost is over. When plants are 7.5cm (3in) high cut out the growing tips to encourage a bushy habit.

Tropaeolum majus _____
Nasturtium

Spread 30cm (12in)
Height 30cm to 1.8m (12in to 6ft)   **HA** ☀ 🐛 ✂ 🌷

Nasturtium is a favourite hardy annual, flowering from early
summer to early autumn, easily grown provided it receives
enough sun and especially popular with children. There are
both dwarf, bushy varieties and climbing kinds. The latter
can also be grown to cascade down a sunny bank, and the
bushy kinds are ideal for sowing in bold groups at the front
of borders.

Good varieties include 'Alaska Mixed', 30cm (12in) high
with a bushy habit and a profusion of brilliant flowers.
'Whirlybird Mixed', 30cm (12in) high, is early flowering and
the blooms face upwards, being held well above the leaves so
that they show up well. There are other separate colours in
the 'Whirlybird' series.

'Jewel Mixed', 30cm (12in) high, produces masses of
semi-double flowers in bright shades of yellow, orange and
red. The 'Gleam' series contains semi-trailing compact
varieties with double or semi-double flowers. All are very
effective in hanging baskets.

Among the climbing or trailing varieties suitable for
covering a bank, there is 'Tall Mixed' or 'Climbing Mixed'.

CULTIVATION
Provide a sunny spot with
well-drained soil. Any kind of
soil is suitable, even
exceedingly poor soils.
Nasturtiums do not mind dry
conditions either.

PROPAGATION
Sow seeds during mid-spring
where the plants are to flower.

Verbena × hybrida (V. × hortensis) _____
Vervain

Spread 30cm (12in)
Height 15–45cm (6–18in)   **HHA** ☀ S ✂ 🌷

Vervain can be mass planted, used as an edging or grown in
tubs, window boxes and hanging baskets.

Varieties are available in mixtures and in separate colours.
There are plenty to choose from in the catalogues, including
'Blaze', 20cm (8in) high, with vivid scarlet blooms on
compact plants. This is an excellent variety for bedding out.
'Showtime', 25cm (10in) high, is a mix of bright colours, the
plants having a spreading habit – ideal for containers.
'Springtime', 25cm (10in) high is extremely colourful and
early flowering, with a dwarf but spreading habit, making it
suitable for containers. 'Tropic', 25cm (10in) high, has deep
crimson flowers.

Verbena aubletia 'Perfecta', 25cm (10in) high, is well worth
growing. The compact rounded plants are exceedingly free
flowering and the colour is a pleasing shade of bright rose.

V. venosa (V. rigida) grows up to 30–45cm (12–18in) in
height and has slender upright stems carrying heads of
purple flowers all summer and into autumn. It is particularly
useful as a foil for other plants.

CULTIVATION
Grow in a sunny position with
well-drained fertile soil.
Regularly remove dead flowers
to encourage more blooms to
follow.

PROPAGATION
Sow seeds under glass or
indoors during late winter or
early spring and transplant
seedlings to trays. Harden
thoroughly and plant out when
the danger of frost is over.

Viola × wittrockiana
Garden Pansy

Spread 20cm (8in)
Height 15–22cm (6–9in)

HHA HB

Garden Pansies are highly popular and not difficult to grow. They are as much at home in cottage gardens as in modern plots and there are varieties that bloom in summer as well as winter/spring.

Best effects are achieved by mass planting them in beds or at the front of borders. Winter/spring flowering kinds associate well with bulbs and other spring bedding plants.

Garden pansies are ideal, too, for containers such as tubs and window boxes.

There is a wide range of varieties and mixtures to choose from, as well as separate colours. Some varieties have an attractive black 'face' to each flower.

Recommended summer-flowering varieties include 'Majestic Giants Mixed', vigorous and early flowering with large blooms in a wide range of colours; 'Imperial Pink Shades', bright pink, fading to pale pink then white; 'Imperial Orange Prince', deep pure orange; 'Imperial Sky Blue', azure blue; and 'Roggli Giants Mixed', with large flowers in a wide range of colours.

Good winter-flowering Pansies include 'Floral Dance Mixed', in a wide range of colours; and 'Universal Mixture', in an equally good colour range.

Violas are also well worth growing. They have Pansy-like blooms but are much smaller. They flower from spring to autumn, attain a height of about 15cm (6in), and can be treated as half-hardy annuals or biennials. Try 'Prince Henry', small purple flowers with gold markings; and 'Prince John', clear bright yellow without markings. Grow violas on the rock garden or plant drifts in the shrub border. Also use them for edging beds and borders.

CULTIVATION
Pansies and Violas like a position in sun or partial sun and a moisture-retentive fertile soil. Add bulky organic matter to light sandy or chalky soils.

PROPAGATION
Pansies and Violas can be grown as half-hardy annuals or as biennials. To grow as half-hardy annuals sow under glass or indoors during early spring, transplant to trays and plant out before they become overcrowded, after hardening thoroughly. Winter-flowering Pansies should be sown in early summer and ideally raised in a cold frame. Transplant into a nursery bed and plant in flowering positions in autumn. To grow Pansies and Violas as biennials make the sowing in a cold frame or outdoors in early summer and transplant to a nursery bed. Move to flowering positions in autumn.

Viscaria elegans (Lychnis coeli-rosa) _____
Rose of Heaven

Spread 15cm (6in)
Height 45cm (18in)

HA

Xeranthemum annuum _____
Immortelle

Spread 15–20cm (6–8in)
Height 60cm (24in)

HA

This is perhaps not too well known but worth sowing in bold groups in the annual or mixed border where colourful star-shaped blooms will be produced from early to late summer. The species has pinky purple flowers each with a white centre, but normally a mixture of colours is grown, such as 'All Types Mixed' in soft pastel shades of rose, pink, blue, lavender, lilac, white, etc.

This is one of the everlasting flowers, whose blooms are dried and used for winter decoration. The daisy-like flowers are produced freely in summer and colours include shades of pink, lilac, purple and white. Usually sold in a mixture such as 'Double Mixed' with crested double cornflower-like blooms on long stems.

CULTIVATION
Full sun or partial sun and any ordinary well-drained soil are recommended.

PROPAGATION
Sow seeds in mid-spring where the plants are to flower and thin out the seedlings to the recommended spacing before they become overcrowded. Alternatively, for earlier flowers the following year make a sowing in early autumn where the plants are to flower. You'll get best results if you live in a mild area and your soil is well drained. Plants can be covered with cloches over winter, particularly if your garden is in a cold part of the country.

CULTIVATION
Grow in full sun and in a well-drained soil. Light sandy soils are especially suitable. Reasonably fertile soils give best results, so add fertilizer before sowing. The flowers should be cut for drying immediately they have opened. Bundle them loosely and hang them upside down in a cool dry airy place, out of direct sun, for a few weeks to allow them to become thoroughly dry.

PROPAGATION
Seeds are sown where the plants are to flower during early or mid-spring, and the seedlings thinned to the recommended spacing before they start to become overcrowded.

Zinnia elegans
Zinnia

Spread 30cm (12in)
Height 15–75cm (6–30in)

HHA

Zinnias are highly popular both in Britain and America. They have large daisy-like flowers, usually double, in a wide range of colours and are excellent for cutting. The dwarf varieties are ideal for mass planting in beds and the taller ones can be planted in groups in the mixed or annual border. The flowering period is early summer to early autumn.

There are lots of varieties to choose from and the following can be recommended. 'Big Top Mixed', 60cm (24in) high, won't grow well in Britain but popular in America. It has large cactus-dahlia-like blooms in a wide range of bright colours. 'Carved Ivory', 76cm (30in), also has cactus-dahlia-like flowers but in cream. 'Peppermint Stick Mixed', 60cm (24in) high, is a dahlia-flowered mix with striped, blotched and stippled flowers in all sorts of colours. Extremely eye-catching and ideal for cutting. 'Statefair Double Mixed', 60–76cm (24–30in) high, has huge dahlia-like blooms in shades of red, pink, orange, gold, yellow and cream. 'Wild Cherry', 76cm (30in) high, is a cactus-flowered variety with brilliant cherry-rose blooms. Dahlia-flowered hybrids, 60cm (24in) high, with fully double flowers, which can be strongly recommended are 'Gold Sun', 'Red Sun' and 'Sunshine Mixed' in a wide range of colours.

'Envy', 45cm (18in) high, is an unusual colour – chartreuse green. The blooms are like double-flowered dahlias and are much in demand by flower arrangers. An excellent choice of annual for a green and white planting scheme.

'Border Beauty Rose', 45cm (18in) high, unfortunately will not grow well in Britain but it's popular in America. The flowers are a pinky salmon colour, fully double and ideal for cutting. 'Peter Pan Mixed', 22cm (9in) tall, is excellent for bedding and comes in a range of bright colours such as reds, yellows and pinks. 'Pulcino', 22–30cm (9–12in) high, is a mix of many clear colours and it comes into flower early. An improved version is 'Belvedere' with exceptional weather resistance. 'Thumbelina Double Mixed', 15cm (6in) high, is one of the dwarfest of the bedding zinnias and highly popular on account of its wide colour range and free-flowering nature.

CULTIVATION
Grow zinnias in full sun and fertile well-drained soil. Work in plenty of manure or compost and add fertilizer before planting. Remove dead flowers to encourage more blooms.

PROPAGATION
Sow under glass or indoors during early spring, transplant to small pots, harden well and plant out when the danger of frost is over. Or sow outdoors during late spring where the plants are to flower and thin out the seedlings before they become overcrowded.

Flower Gardeners' Reference

Annuals and biennials are easily grown and have minimal needs. Keen gardeners, who spend much time tending them will achieve spectacular results; less assiduous gardeners who give their plants minimum attention will, however, still get very good results. The following tips will help you to raise and grow plants well.

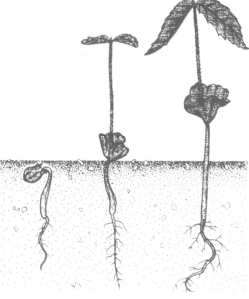

Soils

All soil types are suitable for annuals and biennials provided they are not waterlogged, but most need regular attention to ensure plants flourish.

Digging The best preparation for new beds and borders is digging to two depths of the spade (double digging). If you have the energy, do this where possible every three years. In the intervening years single digging to the depth of the spade will suffice. Dig in autumn ready for spring sowing and planting; or for autumn planting of spring bedding plants.

Alternative to digging Of course, not everyone wants to dig beds; indeed, it may not be possible among permanent plants. So simply fork over the area to be sown or planted to a depth of a few inches, at the same time adding soil improvers (see below), mixing them into the surface.

Improving the soil All soils benefit from the addition of bulky organic matter such as well-rotted manure, garden compost, peat, leafmould, spent hops, spent mushroom compost or pulverized bark. Heavy soils with poor drainage (e.g. clays) benefit from the addition of coarse horticultural sand or grit.

Add these to the trenches while digging, or fork them into the top few inches of soil.

Preparations for sowing outdoors Break down roughly dug soil with a fork. Consolidate by treading. Apply general-purpose fertilizer. Then rake in several directions to break down the soil finely and create about 2.5cm (1in) of loose soil. Prepare soil only when it's dry on the surface but moist below.

The preparation for planting out young plants is the same as for sowing outdoors.

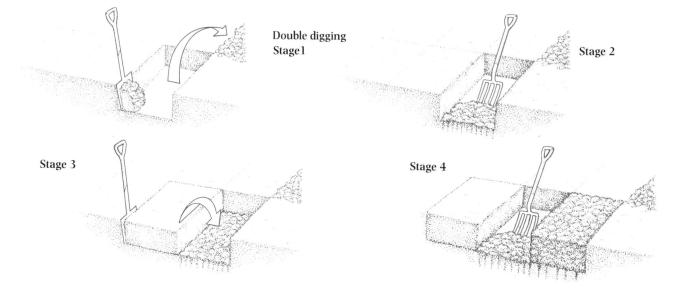

Double digging
Stage 1

Stage 2

Stage 3

Stage 4

Raising and Growing
Hardy Annuals

These are sown in early to late spring in the beds or borders where they are to flower. The state of the soil will dictate exact timing: don't sow when it's cold and wet.

Some hardy annuals can be down in early autumn for earlier blooms next year, provided your garden is in a relatively mild area with well-drained light soil.

Sowing technique Sow each type of annual in a bold informal group – an area of at least 90 × 90cm (3 × 3ft). Sow the seeds in rows of parallel drills or furrows across the area. Spacing of drills varies from about 15cm (6in) apart for small annuals up to 30cm (12in).

Make the shallow drills with a pointed stick or with the corner of a hoe. Most seeds will be happy in 12mm (½in) deep drills. Sow seeds thinly by trickling them between finger and thumb. None should be touching. Then draw fine soil over them and firm it lightly with the back of a rake if the soil's light and sandy.

Water the seed bed after sowing only if the soil is drying out. You should ideally sow into moist soil. Use a fine sprinkler for watering.

Thinning seedlings Before they become too large seedlings should be thinned out to their correct distance apart. Do a preliminary thinning when seedlings have formed their first true leaves and a second and final thinning when the remainder have further developed but are not yet quite touching each other.

Pull out surplus seedings by hand, placing the fingers of your other hand over the soil around the adjacent seeding that is to remain to prevent it being disturbed. Water remaining seedlings after thinning.

Supporting plants Rain and wind can flatten tall and thinned-stemmed annuals, and supports should be provided to prevent damage. The best supports are twiggy sticks pushed into the ground among and around the plants before they get too tall. The sticks should finish slightly below the ultimate flowering heights of the plants.

Metal plant supports are also suitable for annuals and come in various designs and sizes. Yet another method is to insert three or four bamboo canes around each group and to loop thin gardeners' string around them, to encircle and hold in the stems.

General care Water all annuals in dry weather, applying enough to moisten the soil to a depth of at least 15cm (6in).

The removal of dead flower heads before seeds set is recommended; this encourages more flowers to follow on many plants. Cut them off with flower scissors, leaving virtually all of the flower stems.

At the end of the summer or early in the autumn the display will be over and the plants will start to die, so pull them up and put them on the compost heap. Then dig or fork the bed.

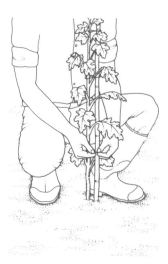

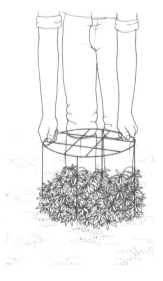

Supporting flowers

Raising and Growing
Half-Hardy Annuals

In temperate (coolish) climates, as in the UK and much of the USA, half-hardy annuals are ideally sown in a frost-free, heated greenhouse or indoors between mid-winter and mid- or late spring according to the plants' growth rates. Slow growers are sown earliest. See also Raising plants indoors.

Sowing techniques Seeds can be sown in full- or half-size seed trays with a depth of 2.5–3.8cm (1–1½in). Use a proprietary soil-based or peat-based seed compost. Firm the compost in the tray with a wooden presser to ensure a smooth level surface on which to sow.

Do sow thinly, so that no seeds are touching. Tiny seeds can be mixed with fine dry silver sand to make sowing easier. Sow the mixture from the palm of one hand, tapping it with the other to slowly release the seeds so that they scatter evenly over the compost surface.

Don't cover tiny seeds with compost but lightly press them into the surface with a wooden presser.

Sow larger seeds in the same way but don't mix them with sand. Very large ones can be spaced out individually. Sift a layer of fine compost or grit over larger seeds. The depth should equal twice the diameter of the seeds.

Then stand the trays in water almost up to their tops until the surface of the compost becomes moist. Add a fungicide to the water to prevent damping-off disease.

Germination conditions The seeds will need a steady temperature of 16–21°C (65–70°F) to germinate. Heat is best provided from below, as with an electrically heated propagating case. Alternatively stand trays on a bench in a heated greenhouse or above a radiator in the house, and cover each with a sheet of glass. When seedlings appear provide maximum light but shade from sun. An ideal minimum temperature to maintain for growing on is 10°C (50°F).

Transplanting seedlings When large enough to handle easily transplant seedlings to other trays to give them room to grow. Trays ideally should be 5–7.5cm (2–3in) deep. Fill them with proprietary soil-based or peat-based-potting compost.

Space out the seedlings an equal distance apart each way in the trays. A standard-size tray will hold 40 seedlings (five rows of eight). Hold seedlings by the seed leaves and plant in holes made with a pencil or dibber, ensuring each seedling is inserted almost up to its lowest leaves. Firm in gently. Larger plants like dahlias and pelargoniums are better potted into 7.5cm (3in) pots and later moved on to 12.5cm (5in) pots.

Water in seedlings and place on the greenhouse bench. Keep them shaded and steadily moist.

Raising plants indoors If you don't have a greenhouse the plants can be raised indoors. Germinate the seeds in an airing cupboard or in any warm room on a windowsill; a windowsill above a radiator is ideal.

Seedlings must be moved to a light position as soon as germination occurs. Turn the trays regularly to prevent the plants from bending towards the light.

Hardening the plants Before planting outside, the plants must be acclimatized to outdoor conditions. Transfer the trays to a garden frame or a light, protected porch two to three weeks prior to final planting.

Close the frame at night to protect plants from frost or bring the trays indoors to an unheated room. Prior to final

Sowing and hardening off

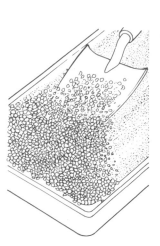
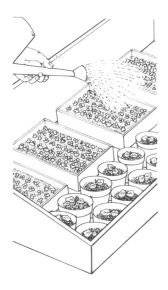

planting, when danger of night frost is over, the night protection should be stopped for a few days.

Buying half-hardy annuals If you buy plants from a garden centre, wait until you are ready to plant, and danger of frost is over.

Good-quality plants should be well hardened; should look sturdy with good, green foliage; and have some flowers plenty of flower buds to follow. Avoid weak spindly plants with pale or blotched leaves. Avoid also plants that have outgrown their containers (yellowing or reddish leaves indicate nutrient deficiency).

Planting out Plant when all danger of frost is over – frost can kill half-hardy annuals.

Containers such as tubs, urns, window boxes and hanging baskets should be filled with soil-based or peat-based potting compost. First put a layer of drainage material in the bottom. Wire hanging baskets should first be lined with sphagnum moss or a proprietary liner, and trailing plants can be planted through the wires and moss in the sides as you fill with compost.

Water plants and containers thoroughly the day before planting out. Gently separate plants in trays by pulling the roots apart or easing them apart with a hand fork. Don't let roots dry out; and make sufficiently large planting holes, with a trowel, to accommodate to roots without cramping. Firm in well with your fingers then water in.

General care When the plants have produced their first flush of flowers you can start a light liquid feeding – not too much or you'll get too much foliage at the expense of flowers. Feeding about once a month will be sufficient, using a proprietary general-purpose or flower-garden fertilizer, high in potash and low in nitrogen for maximum flower production.

Keep plants well watered during dry periods. It's best to use a fine sprinkler, and to apply enough to penetrate to a depth of at least 15cm (6in). Containers must be checked daily (or even twice daily in very hot weather) because they can dry out rapidly.

Regularly remove dead flower heads because this encourages more blooms.

Hanging baskets

Raising and Growing
Hardy Biennials

Most hardy biennials are sown outdoors from late spring to early summer in a prepared seed bed. But very small seeds are best sown in seed trays.

Sow in rows and when seedlings are large enough to handle easily transplant them to a nursery bed to give them room to grow. Plant in rows 30cm (12in) apart with at least 20cm (8in) between seedlings.

Seedlings raised in trays should be pricked out into other trays (as explained for half-hardy annuals) then, before they become overcrowded, transplanted to a nursery bed in the open as outlined above.

The young plants should be kept well watered in dry weather and free from weeds.

Buying plants Hardy biennials can also be bought as young plants from garden centres. The spring and early summer flowering varieties will be available in the autumn.

Some, such as wallflowers, may be sold 'bare-root' in bundles. However, make sure the roots are well wrapped and not dried out. Plant 'bare-root' plants immediately you get them home to prevent roots from becoming dry. Don't buy these plants if the leaves are going yellow as this indicates they have been bundled for too long. Most hardy biennials, however, are sold in trays or strip containers.

The difference between half-hardy annuals and biennials is that the latter will flower in the year after they are bought.

To work out the number of plants you need bear in mind that wallflowers are planted about 30cm (12in) apart each way, so you will need about 16 plants to fill 1m² (1 sq yd). Other smaller plants such as forget-me-nots (myosotis), double daisies (bellis), polyanthus and pansies are planted about 20cm (8in) apart each way, so you will need about 25 plants per m².

Final planting The young plants are set out in their flowering positions in early to mid-autumn, when they should be quite large. Ensure beds and borders are well prepared.

Carefully lift home-grown plants from the nursery bed, and try if possible to retain some soil around the roots. Take out good-sized holes, firm the plants well in, and water.

General care Plants should be checked during winter because a hard frost can partially lift them out of the soil. Re-firm these plants thoroughly.

Large containers do not often dry out and they can be insulated with dry straw or bracken to prevent the compost from freezing and harming the plants, but they should be checked if conditions are bad.

**Pricking out seedlings
raised in trays**

Pests, Diseases and Weeds

Pests Aphids – blackfly and greenfly – may attack the leaves and shoot tips of many plants. When noticed spray plants with a systemic insecticide, such as one containing dimethoate or a combination of permethrin and heptenophos.

Slugs and snails go for any soft plant material, and seedlings and young plants are the most vulnerable. Sprinkle slug pellets, containing methiocarb or metaldehyde, around plants.

Flea beetles attack the leaves of several bedding plants, resulting in masses of small holes. Spray at the first sign of an attack with a systemic insecticide as for aphids.

Caterpillars of various kinds may be found eating holes in leaves, in which case treat the plants with derris dust.

Diseases Club-root disease attacks members of the cabbage family, including ornamental cabbages, wallflowers and stocks. It causes the roots to swell and become deformed, and produces stunted top growth. Preventive treatment involves club-root dip containing thiophanate-methyl, which should be used on the roots of growing plants before planting out.

Wilts and rots – there are several fungal diseases that can cause roots and stems to collapse and/or rot. Plants growing in poor soil conditions are most vulnerable. Try to prevent trouble by improving the soil and treating it with a fungicidal drench of thiophanate-methyl. Dead plants, or dead parts of plants, should be removed and burnt to prevent diseases from spreading.

Rust appears as rust-coloured spots on the leaves of several plants, including hollyhocks. Spray the plants with a fungicide containing copper or propiconazole.

Mildew appears as white powdery patches on leaves and shoot tips of may plants. Grey mould or botrytis can cause rotting of flowers, particularly during a wet summer. Cut off

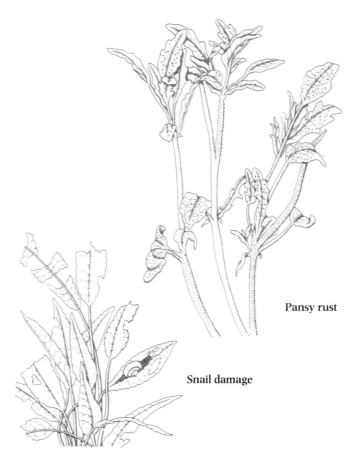

Pansy rust

Snail damage

and burn affected flowers before the disease spreads to healthy parts of the plants. Both diseases can be controlled by a systemic fungicide such as benomyl.

Weeds Weeds must be kept under control at all times because they compete with cultivated plants for food, moisture, air and light. So start off with weed-free beds.

Control seedling weeds among cultivated plants by hoeing them on a dry warm day when the soil surface is dry. The weeds will then quickly dry up and die. To prevent the germination of weed seeds for up to eight weeks, sprinkle propachlor granules over the soil between and around the cultivated plants. The soil must be free from weeds before applying the granules.

Cleaning empty beds of perennial weeds involves spraying with a herbicide containing glyphosphate. And annual weeds can be cleared with paraquate, but again this can only be applied to empty beds.

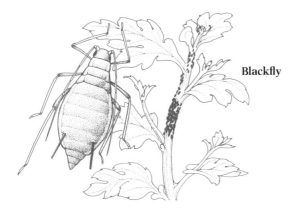

Blackfly

*I*ndex

Acknowledgements

Photographers
HEATHER ANGEL: 29, 31, 33R,
38, 64L, 75R, 94R, 95L; PAT
BRINDLEY: 63L, 71L; LINDA
BURGESS: 28, 59R, 73R;
BRUCE COLEMAN LTD: 73L;
KELLY FLYNN: 31, 66R, 83L,
83R, 86R, 101R; SUE HALL:
40; MARSHALLS SEEDS LTD:
39R, 100L; TANIA MIDGELEY:
37L, 46R, 51L, 53R, 54R, 61L,
64R, 65L, 68, 74R, 77L, 90L;
CLAY PERRY: 28, 29; HARRY
SMITH COLLECTION: 32L, 37R,
40L, 49R, 59L, 65R, 67R, 69,
70L, 76R, 81, 82R, 92R, 102R;
UNWINS SEEDS LTD: 11, 29,
32, 33, 34, 35, 36, 39, 90R,
42, 43, 44, 45, 46, 47, 48, 49L,
50R, 51, 52, 53L, 54L, 55, 56,
57, 58, 60, 61R, 62, 63R, 66L,
67L, 70R, 71R, 72, 74L, 75L,
76L, 77L, 78, 79, 80, 82L, 83C,
84, 85, 86L, 87, 88, 89, 90R,
91, 92L, 93L, 94L, 95R, 96,
97L, 98, 99, 100R, 101L,
102L, 103; MICHAEL WARREN
AIIP: 93R; JEREMY
WHITAKER: 8

Illustrator
NICOLA GREGORY: 1, 3, 5, 7,
10, 11, 13, 14, 15, 16, 17, 18,
19, 20, 21, 22, 23, 24, 25, 26,
27.

T = Top B = Bottom
C = Centre